MW00905673

Please return

Big Al, Zombies, and the Man o the Moon

Big Al, Zombies, and the Man on the Moon

ISBN 978-0-557-94909-0

Dedication

To old and new warriors, especially Big Al.

To all the spouses and families who support and love those warriors.

To Kerry who has a warrior's fortitude.

In memory of my departed son and my muse, Colin Peter.

Table of Contents

Foreword ix

Part I: Big Al, Zombies, and The Man On The Moon 1

Chapter 1:   Hell in the Pacific 1

Chapter 2:   Beginnings 5

Chapter 3:   The Platoon 13

Chapter 4:   The Prisoner 21

Chapter 5:   Big Al 25

Chapter 6:   Personalities 29

Chapter 7:   The First Haircut 35

Chapter 8:   Man on the Moon 37

Chapter 9:   Mobility 39

Chapter 10: Monkeys, Dogs, the Bug Man, and Red Ants 43

Chapter 11: The Bunker 47

Chapter 12: RPGs, Mines, Mortars, and Trees 51

Chapter 13: Detritus 57

Chapter 14: Strange Occurrences 59

Chapter 15: Sheridans 61

Chapter 16: Donut Dollies and Chaplains 65

Chapter 17: Others 67

Chapter 18: Flying with the Air Force 69

Chapter 19: Rome Plows, Rockets, and Helicopter Pilots 75

Chapter 20: Thunder Run 79

Chapter 21: Thanksgiving 81

Chapter 22: Ambush.. 83

Chapter 23: The Hospital 87

Chapter 24: Vietnamization 91

Chapter 25: R&R... 95

Chapter 26: The Watch 97

Chapter 27: Cambodia.. 99

Chapter 28: Fear 103

Chapter 29: Stateside.. 105

Chapter 30: Going Home 107

Part II: The Aftermath.. **111**

Chapter 31: Fort Lewis... 113

Chapter 32: Switzerland 119

Chapter 33: Fort Carson 123

Chapter 34: Fort Leavenworth 133

Chapter 35: West Point 137

Chapter 36: Back to Europe 143

Chapter 37: Hawaii... 157

Chapter 38: Back to Europe Again 161

Chapter 39: Northern Europe 165

Chapter 40: The Last Days in the Army 175

Epilogue 179

Military Glossary 183

Foreword

This is a two-part book. It started as a description of my one-year tour in Vietnam in quasi-chronological order. I have read a number of Vietnam war memoirs and fiction books. They all contain stories of the blood and guts, the glory and the trauma associated with close combat. Certainly, Vietnam had its share of fighting like that. Fortunately, I came back from my tour there in good mental health, or at least with the same mental health I had when I got there. I haven't even had any post-traumatic stress episodes due to the war. However, while visiting the Fort Worth Zoo recently during a Thanksgiving holiday with my two grandchildren, I did experience a Vietnam flashback.

The entryway to the zoo includes a large stand of bamboo. The sound of the bamboo rustling in the wind and its smell gave me a definite sensation of being in the jungles of Vietnam. I physically had to stop my grandchildren Caitlin and Ryan and shake my head to clear the feeling.

This first section of the book deals with none of those iconic episodes made so familiar in print and movies. Instead this book concentrates on the lighter or stranger moments of my tour, for humor (even if it's dark humor) is indeed the best antidote for the serious business of soldiering. All too often soldiering is long periods of boredom punctuated with moments of intense fear and adrenaline. The only way to survive is to laugh at the absurdities of war.

The second part of the book builds upon the first and, like the first, describes how I used the lessons learned in Vietnam and how that worthwhile experience must be passed on to our new soldiers. I think my generation of leaders coming back from Vietnam found its post-war efforts effective in determining the outcome of the first Gulf War. The policies, training, and equipment installed in the aftermath of Vietnam proved themselves in that one hundred-hour fight.

I also found much humor in my army career. The army actually can be a funny place with its cast of characters and broad experiences, especially if you try not taking yourself too seriously.

More importantly, however, Vietnam taught me there is no one like the American soldier. Throughout my subsequent career our soldiers' bravery, fortitude, and compassion continually impressed and heartened me. Be there no doubt, our soldiers demonstrate those same characteristics today for their country. God bless them all.

****

I would like to thank my daughter, Megan, and son-in-law, Doug, for the impetus for this book. I would also like to thank my son, Sean, and daughter-in-law, Mandy, for their interest and support. If no one but my children and grandchildren read it, it will have been a success. Most of all, I would like to acknowledge my beloved wife, Kerry, for putting up with me and my foibles since we first met, likely the best single occasion of my life.

Except in a few instances, I have purposefully omitted names of the platoon members and other soldiers in this tale. They will know who they are and they, in their anonymity, represent the best of the American Army.

Part I

Big Al, Zombies, and The Man On The Moon

Chapter 1

Hell in the Pacific

Individual replacement troops gathered and flew from Travis Air Force Base, California, near Sacramento, to Vietnam, usually in charter aircraft. Most of the soldiers on my flight had never served in Vietnam and seemed very young. The flight departed on June 5, 1969, exactly one year from my graduation from the United States Military Academy at West Point and my commissioning as an Armor second lieutenant.

A civilian charter Trans World Airlines Boeing 707 with airline seats and real stewardesses delivered us to Vietnam. We flew from Travis to the island of Guam in the western Pacific for a short refueling stopover and crew change. We deplaned the aircraft and walked around the military terminal and, for most of us, got our first taste of tropical weather and heat.

The next and final leg of the flight took us into Bien Hoa Air Base outside of Saigon. During this last leg the crew showed us an in-flight film. *Hell in the Pacific* starred Lee Marvin and the Japanese actor Toshiro Mifune. The film had first appeared in the U.S. in December 1968, but I had never heard of it.

The film concerns two fighting men, an American and Japanese, who are marooned on an uninhabited Pacific island during World War II. As enemies, after initial skirmishes, they must accept their differences and work together, despite their two countries being at war. The irony of showing this movie to troops on their way to Southeast Asia never dawned on the flight crew. If that realization occurred did, it certainly didn't stop them.

We sat packed in the crowded cabin, watching or trying to avoid the in-flight movie. We barely understood much of the dialogue, because Mifune only spoke in Japanese with subtitles and Marvin mumbled his lines. The whole situation seemed surreal. Our future in Vietnam occupied most of us.

Before we landed at Bien Hoa Air Base near Saigon, we flew over the lush green of Southeast Asia, so reminiscent of *Hell in the Pacific*. We then loaded on a bus and drove through the bustle of urban Vietnam to the army's replacement depot. During the entire bus ride I wondered as a newbie (a polite version of the names given to newly arrived troops) why we did not have weapons and why the bus had no guards. Any of the many minibus drivers or moped cyclists could have heaved a grenade in the bus' open windows, but the trip turned out to be uneventful. The hot and humid ride seemed to last a long time while we took in the different the smells of Southeast Asia. I had traveled the United States and Europe as an army brat, but had never encountered an environment so totally different: smaller people, pungent odors of fish and strange vegetables, a different kind of bustle, and vibrant colors everywhere.

The stay at the replacement depot, thankfully, was short. The depot basically consisted of dusty temporary barracks structures, half plywood, half mosquito netting, with a canvas roof. Since the base in Bien Hoa had suffered mortar attacks, the sides of the barracks were protected with sandbags up to the height of the plywood. A huge single bay with fold-up cots occupied the inside the building. No one anticipated any soldiers staying at the replacement depot very long. Since no significant loss of lieutenants had occurred in the last few days, I received my assigned as scheduled to the 11th Cavalry Regiment. I flew out the next day to Blackhorse (the regiment's nickname) base camp near Xuan Loc, east of Saigon. There I became a member of the regiment's 1st Squadron. I still had to undergo additional in-country training.

I went to that training, called Blackhorse University, for exactly one day and said "Enough!" I could not endure further delay and reported to the squadron headquarters. As it happened, the squadron commander had just flown in from the field, and I reported to his spartan office for an initial interview.

Major "Doc" Bahnsen was a force to be reckoned with. A big man, with a slight, good ole boy accent, Doc was on his second tour and a favorite of the regimental commander, Colonel George Patton, son of General "Blood and Guts" Patton of World War II fame. Doc had an enviable war record and had demonstrated his fighting attitude and bravery again and again. His first question threw me.

"Where did you graduate in your class at West Point?" he asked a fellow West Pointer.

I allowed as how I graduated as a 'star man' (near the top of the class), thinking Doc would be impressed. In fact, I was a "goat" star man, the last in the group of 35 senior cadets to receive academic stars. In either case, Doc was underwhelmed.

"I don't think a lot of smart guys—they don't know how to fight!" he yelled and then took off on a tirade. He questioned my abilities and motivation, and if he had had more time, would have questioned my ancestry—me, a volunteer to his unit, wanting to fight, and getting nothing but grief for it. I had not been pummeled like that since my first year as a plebe at West Point!

"Get your gear and meet me at the helicopter pad. You're going to Charlie Troop. God help them!"

We did not talk on the helicopter ride out to C Troop. We flew over some rice paddies where I saw my first water buffalo, but the view out the open door of the helicopter was mostly hot, thick jungle—lush and green but interspersed with bomb craters, defoliated areas, and napalm burns.

Charlie Troop consisted of three armored cavalry platoons and a headquarters, approximately one hundred and twenty-five people in the field. As we arrived in the late twilight of the day, the troop occupied its night defensive position. We jumped off the helicopter and Doc introduced me to my new troop commander, Captain Art West. West called forward the 3rd Platoon sergeant and sent me on my way, telling me he would brief me later. It had taken me twenty-two years, but I had finally arrived where I needed to be.

One final event occurred that same day, however, that further introduced me to Vietnam.

As we walked over to the platoon, a CH-47 cargo helicopter flew over us at roughly one thousand feet altitude. For unknown reasons out of the back dropped a large object. As it plummeted closer to the ground, it appeared to be a steel fifty-five gallon drum.

The drum hit the ground right outside our perimeter and burst, spewing a cloud of fine gray spray. It turned out to be tear gas powder employed to deny the enemy reuse of their bunkers. It drifted with the wind over our position and everyone gave up any thought of the enemy or any other tasks while they dug deeply into their gear to find gas masks. Items were heaved out of the troop's armored personnel carriers and tanks as soldiers frantically searched for protection against the tear gas. Soldiers were gasping and wheezing and vomiting.

Ultimately the troop had to move about a kilometer away, upwind of the gas attack. This relocation meant a lot of work, because it necessitated reestablishing the night defensive perimeter with all its associated tasks as it grew dark.

Between the movie, the ass chewing, and the gas attack, what a welcome to Vietnam!

Chapter 2

Beginnings

My one-year tour in Vietnam actually started when I was born. My father, a career military officer, an artilleryman, had served in World War II. He met my mother-to-be in Northern Ireland where his unit trained for the Normandy invasion of Europe in 1944. When the war ended, he brought my mom to the States and they married shortly thereafter. I was born in 1947. My dad reentered civilian life as a civil engineer with the Indiana State Highway Department but rejoined the military shortly thereafter, finally retiring in 1967 as a full colonel.

As an army family, we moved a lot, to Europe and all over the United States. I really only knew the army and found myself heavily influenced by military shows in the early days of television like *The West Point Story* and *Combat* and all the John Wayne movies. We enjoyed the travel and living in a new home and seeing new things every two or three years.

When I graduated from high school I wanted to go to West Point but was not yet old enough. Garnering a scholarship to the Military College of South Carolina, The Citadel, I entered the rough and tumble world portrayed in the novel, *The Lords of Discipline*, at only sixteen. After a year at The Citadel and having been accepted by West Point, I ultimately entered the United States Military Academy in July 1964, thus ensuring myself two freshman ("plebe") years in a row.

There were obviously lots of trials at West Point, but it quickly became clear to me that lying low could prevent a lot of troubles. Near the beginning of Beast Barracks, the summertime testing of new cadets at West Point, our new cadet company underwent training drills to test our knowledge of proper uniform ware and how to quickly get into them. Luckily for me, the Citadel uniforms except for the shape of the dress coat buttons were almost exactly the same and called by similar names. Hence, when cadet cadre announced the next uniform at the drill, I knew exactly what it was and could quickly and properly don it. My plebe roommates would have to look the uniform up in the cadet regulations book and then put it on. While I did help them, my previous year's experience allowed me to perform the process more efficiently than they could—too efficiently, I learned.

Getting my roommates started, I dressed in the new uniform and headed to my place in ranks. The instant I got out the door to my barracks, I saw no other new cadets outside and the training cadre waiting for me. I couldn't turn around; I knew what was coming. I stood at attention in my designated spot, drawing the undivided attention of the cadre, who looked and waited for something to do or someone to harass. Talk about feeling like the dung at a beetle convention!

The cadre lit into me in droves. "How did you get outside so quickly?" "Are you former military?" I gave the plebe cadet's required responses of "Sir, I do not know" and "No, Sir." Needless to say, these answers satisfied no one and the cadre dug more deeply.

"Did you go to a military school?" they asked.

"Yes, Sir!" I responded.

"Where?" they yelled.

Based on the new plebe's protocol, I could not respond that question directly but had to ask them for permission to answer.

"Sir, may I make a statement?"

I immediately received permission and then the proverbial manure hit the fan.

"Sir, The Citadel," knowing what would happen next, for West Point played The Citadel as its first opponent on the fall football schedule.

"So, New Cadet Baerman, are you some kind of Citadel spy?" they queried.

For the next several minutes the throngs continued to gather around me, each cadet taking his opportunity to feast on the lone new cadet who hailed from The Citadel. Finally, other plebes started to show up in the formation area in various states of disrepair based on their interpretation of the uniform to be worn, taking the pressure off me at last.

From that moment, whenever we had one of these uniform drills, I made sure my roommates were completely and properly dressed. Then we all headed out at the same time.

****

I actually enjoyed my years at West Point, once the second plebe year ended. Best of all, I met my future wife, Kerry Ann Harrigan, on a blind date in my second year at West Point. Of course, she had a date with another cadet, but that's a whole different book. We have been together ever since.

Graduating in June of 1968, I actually worried that the Vietnam war would be over before I had a chance to prove myself. Funerals were regularly being held in the West Point chapels for graduates known and unknown to me who were killed in Southeast Asia, but I put these in the back of my mind.

Early in the second semester of my senior year, all my classmates gathered in one of the large auditoriums to select our branch in the army and our first assignment. I picked Armor and the 11th Armored Cavalry Regiment in Vietnam, with a brief stopover in the 6th Armored Cavalry Regiment at Fort Meade, Maryland, for training.

****

At that time all combat arms officers after graduation from West Point had to go to Ranger School, based out of Fort Benning, Georgia. Ranger School then lasted eight weeks and one day—consisting of pure hell, sleep deprivation, and meager (if any) rations. Although we had to be in good condition to go to Ranger School, almost everyone there lost a lot of weight. Some student Rangers got so hungry they even had nightmares about being attacked by cheese burgers. However, the award of the Ranger tab for wear on the left shoulder of my uniform made me proud and indicated the capstone of training for war, of knowing just how far I could push myself and others. The leadership skills I learned there have been permanently chiseled in my brain and I call upon them still.

I have been asked since just how difficult Ranger School was. My reply has been steadfast since my tour in Vietnam and is probably the same for all Ranger graduates. If given the choice of going back to Vietnam for a year, despite the danger of being shot at and killed, or doing Ranger School again, I would have picked the Vietnam tour.

After Ranger School, I drove up in my 1968 Pontiac GTO with New York plates through Alabama north to Fort Knox, Kentucky. This was the presidential election year in which Alabama's governor, George Wallace, campaigned for president. I had just crossed the border into Alabama from Georgia when the local police pulled over me for speeding.

A police officer who reminded me of *Smokey and the Bandit* got out of his cruiser. "Boy, let me see your registration and license."

"Officer, I really don't think I was speeding," I said mindlessly.

"Don't you give me any lip," said Smokey. Suddenly I found myself in the back of his police car. Thoughts went quickly through my head of floundering in a backwoods Alabama jail, never to be seen again.

"New York boy, eh?" Smokey looked none too happy. The days of northerners coming down south as Freedom Riders popped into my historical consciousness. "Ya'll got any ID?"

In probably the best move I have ever made, I pulled out my brand new second lieutenant identification card. "Why, son, why didn't you tell me you was in the army? We take care of our soldiers down here."

I proceeded quickly to explain I had just graduated from Ranger School on my way to Fort Knox before going to Vietnam. "Boy, you're really lucky," replied Smokey. "I'm just goin' to give you a ticket."

That fifty dollar ticket, paid in cash, totaled forty-five dollars in court costs and five dollars for speeding. I am sure the fine was deposited directly into the George Wallace campaign fund. Nevertheless, it was also a wise investment to set me free.

The next day, I got up in the morning to complete the drive to Fort Knox. Still suffering the lingering privations of Ranger School, I went to the diner attached to the motel. The waitress came with the breakfast menu. I looked at it briefly and simply ordered one of everything, about six items total.

"Ya'll just out of Ranger School, ain't ya?" was all she said.

****

I visited Kerry once during my stay at Fort Knox, Kentucky, for training at the officer's basic course. During the course I spent one weekend at Kerry's family home. Kerry tells me now that she practically didn't recognize me after the rigors of Ranger School and that I acted oddly. The thought passed through her mind that perhaps I wanted to get out of our impending wedding. She now realizes that post-Ranger School shock, trying to catch up on sleep, still emaciated, and weary to the bone all affected me that weekend.

Thankfully, Kerry and I married on time in December at Saint Brigid's Church in Westbury, New York. After a honeymoon to the

Bahamas, I reported to the 6th Armored Cavalry Regiment (because the unit had a unicorn on its shoulder patch the soldiers called it "the Horny Horse'), just outside Washington, D.C. Army policy stated that lieutenants had to spend at least four months stateside with a regular army unit before reporting to Vietnam. I received assignment to I Troop in mid-December 1968.

My adventures with the 6th Cavalry began with my introduction to my new troop commander, a veteran of Korea and Vietnam who had two middle initials, "V.C." Was this an omen about my eventual assignment?

Preparation for Vietnam in the 6th Cavalry consisted of hours of standing at attention guarding the White House from demonstrators during President Nixon's first inauguration, keeping coal-fired boilers going in old World War II wooden barracks at Fort Meade, and riot control drills and duty in Washington, D.C. as the war progressed into early 1969.

I did learn from riot control duty that not even tear gas could keep a good drunk down. During riot duty we did not have the manpower to post guards on every important building as we patrolled the Washington precinct we had been assigned. Therefore we would periodically throw tear gas canisters into buildings we wanted to keep people out of, including liquor stores. During one round, we heard noises coming from one of these liquor stores. Putting on our protective masks to filter out the tear gas, we went into the building. Near the back we found an old wino, crying his eyes out from the tear gas, but still holding a half full bottle of Jim Beam. We finally had to carry him out of the building because we feared for his health— whatever that meant.

In April of 1969 I did get an opportunity to take the troop's mortars down to Camp Pickett, Virginia, where the Vietnam veterans who only had a short time remaining in the army played with their new lieutenant. We planned to live-fire the troop's three mortars and have the unit's scouts observe and adjust the rounds as they impacted near selected targets.

We fired the rounds down range into the impact area, but no explosions were seen or heard. We fired another volley with the same result. After inspecting the weapons, I heard snickering in the background. Seeing my army career ending before it really began, I pulled a sergeant aside.

"What's going on?"

"With what, sir?" he answered with a straight face.

"The mortars—where did the rounds go?"

Everyone around the mortar firing point stood quietly like utter innocents. Then they burst out laughing, having pulled a good one on the new lieutenant. It turned out they had fired the rounds without screwing on the detonator fuzes. Although the rounds impacted in approximately the right spot, there could be no explosions.

The mortarmen had a good joke and the lieutenant learned a few lessons! The crews properly assembled the rest of the rounds. I ensured the remainder of the firing exercise went well and the training was completed successfully.

****

After my requisite time with the unit, I left Fort Meade in early May and took a short leave. Kerry settled on Long Island, again staying with her parents while she prepared to teach science at John McKenna Junior High School in the fall. In early June 1969 I reported to my port of embarkation, in this case, Travis Air Force Base, California, east of San Francisco.

I climbed on board a Trans World Airlines charter Boeing 707 along with about two hundred other anxious troops for the long ride to Vietnam. Was my training sufficient? Would I be prepared for the first contact? How would I react? Would I be afraid? Would I live up to my alma mater's motto, "Duty, Honor, Country?"

It was time to go to war.

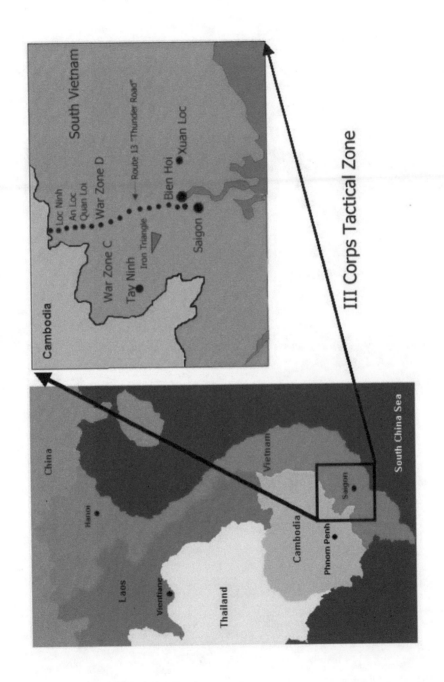

III Corps Tactical Zone

Chapter 3

The Platoon

When I met up with Charlie Troop in early June 1969, it was assigned an area north of Saigon with a mission of conducting reconnaissance-in-force operations. "Reconnaissance-in-Force" (RIF) is a military term for a unit that is conducting a reconnaissance (normally a "look, see, and report" mission with fighting only as necessary), but one in which the unit is prepared to do some heavy fighting. It actually meant days and weeks scouring the jungle based on scanty intelligence as to the enemy's location, looking for the enemy and more intelligence clues. Once you happened upon the enemy, either he began the battle with an ambush or you initiated the fight. The folks we were up against were invariably regular North Vietnamese Army (NVA) troops, and they were superb light infantry. Most of the time you didn't find them until they wanted to be found, or you, by luck, came across one of their base camps.

ACAV

I was assigned as the Third Platoon Leader. Like all the line platoons in the

Sheridan

troop, Third Platoon consisted of nine tracked vehicles (known to us as "tracks"): three light tanks called Sheridans and six Armored Cavalry Assault Vehicles (ACAVs), armored personnel carriers modified with armor around the vehicle commander's station and two side-mounted M60 machineguns.

Each Sheridan had a three-man crew instead of the normal four. Everyone rode on the outside of the Sheridan during operations until a fight started, then the crewman who loaded the main gun ammunition would jump inside to load. The vehicle commander would aim and fire the main gun, eliminating the need for a gunner since most targets were almost within spitting distance. The third crew member, the Sheridan's driver, would keep on the lookout for close-in targets.

Four or five soldiers usually manned each ACAV. The six ACAVs, included four assigned to the scouts, one devoted to carrying demolitions, and one as the platoon leader's vehicle.

Though hardly old myself, it struck me as I met the platoon the young age of the soldiers. Of the thirty-five or so men, only the platoon sergeant and one other sergeant were older than I. I had only turned 22 the previous month. Vietnam was definitely a very young man's war. I would estimate that the average age in the platoon was 19-plus years old.

Big Al Littlejohn was the platoon sergeant, my second-in-command, a staff sergeant with about ten years in the army, about twenty-eight years old. He had been the platoon sergeant for about five months and was extremely capable. He had been stationed as a recruiter previously at the Presidio of San Francisco and was a 6th Army boxing champion. He was well respected by the troops.

It was a draftee army. Although one sergeant, Kurt Wolf, had had some junior college (and had gone through an accelerated training program to make him a "shake and bake" sergeant), I was the only college graduate in the platoon. The platoon was about fifty percent white, thirty percent black, and the remainder Hispanic. Very few were married and fewer yet had any children. The sergeant on the track that carried the demolitions, Earl Sizemore, proudly honored his son by naming the track after him, *Clarence*. All the vehicles in Charlie Troop began with the letter "C," although some names floated about were not permitted due to their pornographic nature.

I was fortunate with my platoon. Big Al kept them in good shape and there were no morale or discipline problems, with one exception (that you will see was capably handled.) We did have our questioners, our gripers, a couple who were looking for glory, and some very quiet individuals. Everyone appeared to want to do his job properly, especially after being counseled by Big Al. What I know for certain, as in past wars, the men in the platoon fought for each other and let the bigger political and military objectives sort themselves out. I know without equivocation these men were primary influences in the rest of my army career (and life for that matter.) There are very few days that go by when I don't think about them and what they taught me.

I only desired to be a good leader and never let my soldiers or platoon down in any way. What I had learned at West Point and The Citadel was one thing, putting it into practice now in a war zone was another.

Big Al, like all good non-commissioned officers (NCOs), wanted to make sure his lieutenant was successful, for the accomplishment of the mission and the welfare of the platoon. He taught his new lieutenant an extremely important lesson right off the bat, one that I had never heard discussed in any of my college psychology of leadership classes. After a fight, at his insistence, he and I always made our way through the platoon talking to each and every soldier and looking them in the eye, followed by a firm grasp of the shoulder or arm. If a soldier shied away from the touch or wouldn't return your look, it meant leadership had to spend more time with him, talking through the battle. There is something about human touch and a caring face that brings soldiers back to the present and heals the mental wounds in the aftermath of a fight. Big Al's wisdom using this technique and imparting it to me right from the start kept all of us going.

The new soldiers reported to the field and remained there for literally their entire tour. They only left the field to go on R&R (rest and relaxation) leave or if they were a casualty who required hospitalization. They spent months on end with their comrades and tracks going through the same routine: morning stand-to in some desolate place before first light; clean up of vehicle, position, and self which primarily consisted of taking in their vehicle's mines, flares, and rocket-propelled grenade (RPG) protective screen; usually a hot breakfast (bacon, eggs, and bread) prepared by the cook who brought out the evening meal and breakfast supplies the night before by helicopter; weapons and vehicle maintenance checks; and burning of any refuse, to include mixing diesel fuel with latrine waste. The troop and platoons then departed on the day's mission, usually a day of boredom but with a constant undercurrent of fear due to a mine or contact with the enemy.

The troop usually maneuvered in the jungle in a series of columns with its platoons abreast, led by the heavier vehicles, usually the Sheridan. Sometimes, if the jungle was particularly dense, the troop would have a platoon of heavy M-48 tanks attached (the M-48 was about three times the weight of a Sheridan) to "bust the jungle." Normally each platoon would be in two columns with the platoon leader right behind his Sheridans. Thus a troop formation might be four to six vehicles on line, i.e., three platoons side by side across a frontage of 150 meters. In another configuration, two platoons might be side by side with the third platoon following, ready to maneuver left or right depending on the contact. Alternatively, in less dense terrain, the scouts in their ACAVs might lead with the Sheridans ready to react. Rarely did platoons go out by themselves on a mission but instead remained within close contact with one another to provide mutual support.

Near the end of the day, hopefully before dark, after riding on the vehicles for hours, the troop would pull into a night defensive position (NDP). The troop would select a place for helicopter resupply, usually adjacent to but sometimes inside the perimeter of the position, and prepare the actual night position itself. The tracks might be arrayed in a one hundred meter diameter circle with all the tracks facing outward. The troop headquarters and the mortars set up in the middle of the circle. Then certain tasks had to be accomplished.

First among these defensive tasks was clearing fields of fire for our weapons by mashing down the undergrowth with our tracks or chopping it down with machetes. Then we would put out trip flares and Claymore anti-personnel mines to warn and protect us of approaching enemy soldiers on foot. The mines and flares would be tied in around the perimeter with the vehicles to the left and right. We would then erect a section of chain link fence on stakes in front of each vehicle to fend off RPGs, probably the most feared weapon the enemy would use against us.

Next, like the cavalry of old, we took care of our horses, the maintenance on the vehicles as required, to include refueling, checking on fluids, small repairs, and cleaning it up after the day's operations. All kinds of leaves and branches would fall on top of or into the track and had to be swept out. The troop's mechanics would start to perform the more complex maintenance tasks, to include, if necessary, replacing major engine and suspension components brought out in resupply. They would often work in difficult conditions through the night in the dark to have a vehicle ready the next morning.

Similarly, the next task included reporting what supplies needed to be replenished on the following day's resupply: ammunition, C-rations, oil, vehicle parts, etc. If the schedule called for a dismounted patrol, the patrol leader (usually a lieutenant) had to make all the preparations and coordination required.

A group of soldiers from the troop's headquarters prepared a landing area for the resupply helicopter (a CH-47 Chinook heavy lift bird) that would bring in whatever had been ordered the previous day. After it had dropped off with its exterior cargo hook its sling load of fuel bladders, a water trailer, and a cargo net full of assorted ammunition, cases of soda, straw-insulated blocks of ice, and other bulky items, it landed nearby with the normal internal load of mail, newspapers, food with a cook, plus small repair parts and any new or returning personnel. Often the resupply bird, because of the weight of items, would make a couple of trips to the field location.

Finally and only then, did we take care of ourselves: personal maintenance: hygiene, writing letters, and relaxing a little before evening stand-to.

If a dismounted patrol was being sent out, those soldiers ate first and made their individual preparations to spend the night outside the NDP at a preselected spot where the enemy might try and approach the perimeter (see *Ambush* later in the book).

The cook who came out on the resupply bird would serve a hot evening meal that had been prepared back at base camp and placed in insulated food containers to one platoon at a time. Meanwhile, the perimeter would remain alert with every heavy machinegun manned.

The day would end with the whole perimeter on alert for evening stand-to. Each track would then revert to one person manning its heavy machinegun for a two to three hour guard shift, waking the next person and taking his place to sleep. On occasions, though not every night, the troop would conduct a "mad minute," firing all the weapons to keep any enemy probes at bay. Periodically throughout the night, the troop's mortars would fire on likely foot avenues of approach. As an aside, the best "mad minutes" took place after dark on Independence Day, July 4th, and New Year's Eve. Every unit in the field in Vietnam would save up its pyrotechnic munitions—parachute flares, colored star clusters, etc.—and fire them off. I'm sure the requests for replacement munitions and pyrotechnics the next day drove the supply folks crazy.

The daily routine could be numbing, but the troopers recognized quickly the importance and discipline of that routine. Their courage and endurance day in and day out in the field over long months amazes me yet.

****

Each vehicle was heavily laden with all types of supplies. The Sheridans had their main gun ammunition plus several thousand rounds of both .50 caliber and 7.62mm machinegun ammunition. The ACAVs were also heavily loaded with ten thousand rounds of .50 caliber and at least an equal amount of M60 ammunition. Each vehicle carried additional spare machineguns and barrels, M16 rifle and .45 caliber pistol ammo, grenades, trip flares, Claymore mines, oil and other lubricants, water cans, an insulated Mermite food container used as an ice chest, C-rations, and cases of soda. Each soldier had a few personal hygiene items, writing supplies, perhaps a camera, and a rain poncho and poncho liner blanket.

Much of the spare material (radios, weapons, and vehicle spare parts) came from tracks that had been damaged or destroyed in combat. The soldiers would salvage anything they could from those tracks and hoard the items until they were needed in the field.

Few of us had any spare uniforms, relying instead on the supply system to send us new clothes as the old ones literally rotted off. We didn't even wear underwear except for T-shirts. That freedom meant less jungle rot and fewer rashes and skin diseases.

****

I had barcly arrived in the platoon before a run-in with my crew occurred. It was during my first fight as I was trying to maneuver the platoon. I couldn't get anyone in the platoon on the radio. I resorted to using hand and arm signals and gestures to convey what I wanted the tracks to do when I noticed both the radio antennas on my track were gone. I spied them sticking up out of the ACAV's cargo hatch.

"Remount the antennas," I yelled at the crew. "I'll talk to you later."

After the fight, the crew and I convened. "What the hell is going on with the antennas?" I barked.

"Sir, the enemy uses the two antennas to aim his RPGs through. They know two antennas mean a command track. We were just thinking of you!"

I thanked them for their concern then tried to convince them of the need to communicate with the rest of the platoon and the troop. They remained adamant in their 'concern.'

Ultimately we compromised. A few days later, with both my antennas and communications in place, I arranged with the troop executive officer to have second dummy antennas placed on every other track in the platoon, thus posing a dilemma for the enemy shooters. The lieutenant wasn't going to be fooled again!

Chapter 4

The Prisoner

Shortly thereafter the squadron moved farther north, away from the Saigon area and toward Cambodia. Word also went out that the squadron commander wanted a prisoner, if we could get one in this new area.

Shortly after relocating, the troop got into a fight. We sometimes had a hard time determining how many North Vietnamese Army soldiers we were fighting until the battle was over, and the area cleared. Moreover, the fights always took place at very close range, perhaps at times no more than twenty-five meters and sometimes even much closer between the enemy and our troops. We would come across each other and a fight would erupt. At times we had danger warning signs, as we found trails or bunkers, but more often firing just began and then the troop leadership tried to figure out which way to maneuver. We would go from a slow ride through the jungle to all hell breaking loose in a split second. Once the fighting broke out it was almost a relief—the constant tension waiting for that to happen was tough.

This particular fight began in a similar fashion and the troop oriented on the enemy force. As the battle continued, I saw my right machinegunner fire at an armed enemy who appeared then went down, apparently wounded. Recognizing the need for a prisoner, I hopped out of the track commander's position and jumped to the ground. I started across a fifty-meter-wide open area to see if I could find the enemy.

As I trotted in front of the line of tracks (remember, I had been in-country only about two weeks), I realized that I had neither a helmet nor a weapon on me. Further, crossing the open space I noticed little tufts of grass and bits of dirt fly into the air. A flash from an old war movie hit me of an airplane strafing a field, causing similar effects, and I even said to myself, "This is just like in the movies!"

However, I picked up my pace, sprinting across the field as the "strafing effect" continued, aiming for the location where the enemy had disappeared. As I approached that point it became further obvious to me that I had no weapon and that the enemy had been carrying an AK-47 rifle.

Sure enough, he brought his rifle to bear on me as I approached. I kicked him in the chest and knocked the rifle away. Our fire had wounded him in the leg and he the worse for wear. Grabbing his rifle and throwing him over my shoulder (he was not very big), I started back across the field. The men in my platoon put down some heavy suppressive fire, and, while I saw the strafing effect again, the trip running back was relatively uneventful.

Big Al had radioed the troop commander that we had a prisoner and Captain West relayed that to squadron. Major Bahnsen then proceeded to land his helicopter right behind the line of vehicles and I carried the prisoner over to him.

I tried to think of something heroic or manly to say, considering how Doc had treated me during our last meeting. Unfortunately, I only weakly uttered, "So there!" as I tossed the wounded prisoner into the back of his helicopter.

Four things happened because of this captured prisoner. First, it turned out the prisoner provided valuable intelligence to the squadron about conditions and enemy dispositions in our new area of operations.

Second, I learned just how dumb it was to ever leave my vehicle without taking the proper precautions, especially not to have a weapon. From then on an M16 rifle hung from my commander's cupola. I would feel its strap as a reminder every time I hoisted myself from my position to dismount from the track.

Thirdly, Doc wrote in his memoirs (*American Warrior*—Citadel Press) that the capture caused him to change his mind about smart guys. He said, "I have to admit my bias against academic types. My experience with the majority of the ones I'd served with was that they wouldn't do anything to get their hands or uniforms dirty."

He then added, "I can still see Baerman and his POW today. He was wearing a sweat-stained T-shirt, no helmet, had an AK-47 in his hand, and came huffing and puffing, dragging a POW behind him, to where I was standing. That was a defining moment that redefined what I thought about 'smart bastards.'"

Finally, and most important, Big Al came over to me as I got back to my track and the fight wound down. I busily chugged down water from a five-gallon can (it is amazing how thirsty a little job can make you!). He pulled me aside.

"LT," (pronounced 'ell-tee', the name for a lieutenant in Vietnam), "you ever pull a stunt like that again and I will personally kill you!"

"I was just getting a prisoner."

"Goddammit! You ran out there naked as a jaybird without any idea what the situation was! I don't get paid to lose a lieutenant right off the bat."

Big Al, of course, was right. Intellectually, I understood that war could kill, but reality hadn't sunk in yet. My tour had barely started and I thought that I was immortal.

****

Later in my army career, I used this prisoner episode to teach lieutenants the importance of proper battlefield attire when you dismount, proper care of a prisoner, and, most especially, spatial awareness on the battlefield—how and where the leader should position himself. Don't be afraid to lead, but also try to avoid terminal dumbness!

Chapter 5

Big Al

Big Al not only performed as a superb platoon sergeant and leader, but he loved technology. When he had the opportunity, he would buy the latest electronic gadget. Three particular incidents involving Big Al and his electronic loves come to mind. Remember, this was a time when the transistor was a big deal and the personal computer was still far in the future. If he hadn't been a boxing champion, I might have almost called him a geek, or whatever the word was at the time, but certainly not to his face.

One day, Big Al came back from a trip to the base camp with a new 8mm movie camera and began using it to film the daily life of operations in the troop. I think he fancied himself a reincarnation of Cecil B. DeMille, the famous Hollywood director. Only a short time passed, however, before Big Al's film-making career came to a head.

We got into a fight and the troop came on line to sweep through a bunker area. Our weapons cleared the way and everything progressed smoothly, as I looked over a couple of tracks and saw Big Al filming the battle and not employing his weapon. He even stood on top of his Sheridan to gain height for his shots and made panoramic sweeps of the battlefield with his movie camera. The tumultuous noise of the battle made it hard to contact him on the radio, so I dismounted and climbed aboard his track.

"What the hell are you doing? Get back on your weapon!" I yelled over the noise.

"I'm getting great shots of the action!" he yelled back, but then relented and stopped filming, jacked back the charging handle on his .50 caliber machinegun and started firing again.

Big Al later sent the film off for development. He premiered it at twilight against a sheet on the troop's command post vehicle. However, he never filmed again in battle.

****

The second incident concerned a TV set. When we stopped our mounted operations, usually in the late afternoon, we found or made an open area where the troop had decent fields of fire for its weapons and where a resupply helicopter could land. While one person remained manning a machinegun on the top of each track, other crewmembers proceeded to perform the routine tasks to prepare the perimeter.

Later, after all the usual preparations had been completed, Big Al would pull out his small battery-powered black and white TV set. If not on battery power, he would hook it up somehow to his vehicle's electrical system if we were in signal range of an Armed Forces Vietnam TV station. It so happened that the Saigon station covered our area of operations.

As it grew dark and before stand-to, Big Al kept the TV on, watching the end of the popular show *Star Trek*. Several soldiers gathered around the top of his Sheridan. The TV set sat propped on top of his .50 caliber machinegun. Out beyond the perimeter a shot was fired and Captain Kirk of the Starship Enterprise took it right between the eyes, exploding the TV set. No one else was hit and we all clamped down on light discipline! I found out later when I got back to the states that Captain Kirk had survived and went on the make *Star Trek* movies.

Needless to say, Big Al did not replace the TV set.

****

The final technological incident found us testing a position-location device. Unlike today's Global Positioning technology, this device used inertial navigation with gyroscopes. The army's Aberdeen Proving Ground had developed it. It was supposed to give us an accurate location in the flat jungle country north of Saigon. I found reading a paper map accurately because there were no real terrain features to orient on. We often used a compass and vehicle odometer to determine where we were. Otherwise, a helicopter overhead could assist giving us our location.

Big Al recognized the value of the device and had volunteered our platoon to test it. It would go on the left rear fender of a scout track. In order to use the device, one would go to a known point on the ground like a road intersection, input the intersection's coordinates, and then head off into the jungle. Periodically the device would need updating, but meanwhile it provided a map readout supposedly accurate within one hundred meters.

The device was mounted on a bracket welded on the rear of the track, so it stood out about a foot. Setting the known point in the device, off we headed into the jungle. The track had gone no more than fifty meters when, in the course of maneuvering, it brushed against a tree and smashed the device to bits.

Big Al was heartbroken and we never saw the device or its successor again. I wonder what Big Al thinks about the electronics revolution now. My family also wonders why I am a technophobe.

****

Big Al lost his leg in a firefight and returned stateside in October 1969 after a stop in a hospital in Japan, a great loss to the platoon. He put me on my feet as a combat platoon leader and demonstrated on so many occasions that the strength of the U.S. Army resides in its non-commissioned officer corps. Staff Sergeant Jesse Crowe, another superb NCO, replaced Big Al as platoon sergeant and the platoon motored on.

When we lost someone in the platoon due to serious injuries, we often would not hear their status unless they wrote back from the hospital and let us know. Unfortunately, due to the individual replacement policy of the army at the time (unlike the more effective and stronger unit replacement policy of today), it was and even had to be "out of sight, out of mind." We just continued on with the war.

Chapter 6

Personalities

While we had young soldiers in the platoon that did not mean their personalities had not fully developed. The platoon consisted of the serious and the comical, the shy and the standouts, and the peculiar who had amazing things happen to them. The troop even had a native Vietnamese in the troop.

My father, a retired colonel and World War II vet, often railed at the tenor of the popular TV show, *MASH*, and its characters. I know, however, that he had folks in his wartime unit just like my soldiers.

****

It seemed all the Sheridan drivers in the platoon, like their vehicles, had their own idiosyncrasies. One soldier wanted to be an entomologist. Another Sheridan driver, Mel LaFranchi, collected Purple Hearts. In fact, he had so many I thought of him as "Iron Ass."

Iron Ass was a good soldier, but he always seemed to intersect with explosions or other shrapnel-producing occurrences. He already had four Purple Hearts by the time I got to the platoon, but none of those injuries required hospitalization.

Shortly after I arrived in the platoon, we departed on a mission after having stopped at the American base camp at Quan Loi, halfway from Saigon to the Cambodian border. The camp had a C-130 fixed wing cargo aircraft dirt strip nearby, which is how it got much of its resupply.

The platoon made an end run around the far end of the airstrip as a C-130 was landing. A well-aimed rocket-propelled grenade (RPG) hit the plane as it touched down and exploded. The explosion happened perhaps one-half mile away, but Iron Ass yelped from his driver's seat and we pulled over to see what the situation had happened. Iron Ass had a small piece of shrapnel that had to have come from the exploding plane sticking out of his neck and blood trickling down onto his T-shirt. I will forever associate the wreckage of the "Quan Loi Queen," which we passed frequently on missions in that area, with Iron Ass. Iron Ass eventually was awarded seven Purple Hearts and made it home safely to the U.S. He must cause fits for Transportation Administration security screeners when he flies.

****

Another wounded soldier, Angel Miranda, came about his Purple Heart in a similarly unbelievable fashion. Crews would keep soda and ice in a Mermite container on their tracks. A Mermite is an insulated container designed to keep food hot or cold in the field after it is prepared in a field kitchen. Normally Mermites with food came out to the troop every evening on the resupply helicopter along with blocks of ice and were returned the next morning for reuse. Yet, somehow, every crew managed to obtain a Mermite for their track, and it was a valued possession.

The heat in Vietnam where we operated was intense and oppressively humid, particularly when wearing a flak jacket. Troops would drink fluids all the time, either Kool-Aid or sodas or, reluctantly, warm water. Canteens full of Kool-Aid and as many sodas as possible were kept in the crew's Mermite container with ice that was brought out with the nightly resupply.

The Mermite container would sometimes rest on the edge of a cargo hatch right behind the track commander's position on top of the track. This would allow easy access to fluids during the day. Once, during a fight, an enemy RPG fired at our track exploded on the Mermite. Ice, water, canteens, fizzing soda cans, and pieces of Mermite spewed everywhere.

Checking on everyone, Angel reported to me that he thought he had been wounded. I leaned over the commander's cupola and saw him bleeding from the neck under his helmet. There on the floor of the driver's compartment was a torn, spinning, frothing soda can of Wink. There was a smudge of blood on it. Although it may be a bit ignominious to be wounded by a can of soda, it was definitely a wound received due to enemy action. I would have gladly awarded the Mermite a medal for giving its life for my crew!

On the next resupply run, the troop cook took back one fewer Mermite can than he flew out with, and we had our replacement.

****

Another Sheridan driver, Ron Mihalenko, had a cleanliness obsession, an odd trait for a soldier who worked with and maintained heavy machinery all day long. He was very fastidious and would bathe in one form or another every day. He always seemed to have a clean uniform, and I can still see him striding across the troop position wearing his flip-flops with a towel around his shoulders having completed his daily hygiene routine.

The rest of us cleaned up about once a week or sooner if we were having a visitor. In the rainy season, during its torrential downpours, it was not unusual to see us stop operations, strip off our clothes on top of our tracks, pull out the soap, and lather up during a rainstorm. I suppose any NVA who may have been observing us thought we were crazy, but it did save on water resupply. It was a bit uncomfortable, however, if the rain stopped abruptly in the middle of our 'showers,' and we remained 'caked up' until the next storm.

Rain showers also caused peculiar things to happen. Because the troop had roughly thirty tracked vehicles, we could raise a cloud of dust even in a rain storm. It was not unusual to have both the troopers and their tracks to be both dusty and covered with mud from the rain at the same time. I would contend that armored troops were probably dirtier in general than other troops in the field because of their tracks and the environment in which they operated.

During the dry season we would use the water in our five-gallon cans and rig a shower using a folding canvas bucket-like device. It had a nozzle on one end, and we would fill the bucket with water, hang it over the side of the track on a pole, stand on a plastic five gallon can turned on its side, and wash away. Though we were out in the open, naked for all to see, it was much more civilized than the rainy season method!

****

In the troop we even had a North Vietnamese Army soldier who acted as an advisor under the Chieu Hoi (Vietnamese for "Open Arms") program. He was a soldier who had surrendered and now worked for us. He was in his late-twenties and had been a soldier for about ten years, the last two for the U.S. Army under the Chieu Hoi program.

He rode with the troop commander but did not participate in any of our fights. His experience with the other side made him particularly useful in picking up signs of enemy activity. He could see and sense things we did not and give us early warning. He would eat our chow (and loved it) and sleep in the track with everyone else.

He had no family in the North and had been with the troop for 18 months. He was content with his job although he was in as much danger as anyone.

We were in the Michelin Rubber plantation during one operation, the first time the troop had operated in this particular area in a while. The rubber trees were planted in rows at regular intervals like orange groves with shallow irrigation ditches running parallel to the trees. It was not unusual to see local rubber workers there, tapping the trees for the milky-white rubber tree resin that would flow into plastic buckets. The nice thing about the rubber trees was the shade they provided as well as their relative openness compared to the jungle.

As we drove down the rows of rubber trees we noticed movement up ahead. One of the scout tracks reported it, followed up by a comment, "They're just rubber workers." Suddenly, however, the Chieu Hoi (as he was called) started getting excited, yelling, "Dinks! Dinks!" Dink was the U.S. Army's derogatory term for an enemy soldier in contrast to Gooks, who were friendly South Vietnamese.

One of the "rubber workers" then reached behind a tree and aimed an RPG at our lead track, bouncing the rocket off the ground and missing his target. Over the radio another scout bellowed, "Rubber workers, hell!" and opened up with his machinegun.

To this day I still don't know how the Chieu Hoi was able to determine the difference between real rubber workers and the enemy imposters.

****

As I mentioned earlier, every track in Charlie Troop had a name that started with the letter "C." Hence, there were tracks named *Cong Crusher*, *Cav Country*, *Courageous*, etc. However, there was one Sheridan crew who wanted to name their replacement vehicle (their earlier one had been destroyed by an RPG and subsequent fire) *Snow White*. A peculiar name indeed until you consider that the three young soldiers aboard were all African-American and, moreover, not exactly "teasing tan," as they said.

The year, remember, was 1969, at the height of the Black Power movement, and they wanted to show some solidarity, with a sense of irony, with their brothers at home. Rules were rules, however, and the name had to start with a "C" and be stenciled on the side of the vehicle. They acquiesced and named the vehicle *Congo*.

The purpose of this story is much deeper. It did not take very long, usually after the first enemy contact, for the new guys to blend in and for everyone to become literally the same color. The brotherhood of war, the danger, the smell of the jungle and ourselves, and the color of the Vietnamese mud and dust made us one. If you look at any pictures from Vietnam you will see, particularly among those units who churned up a lot of dust like the 11th Cavalry, only one color of skin. It is a medium brown with a reddish tinge and permeated everyone's clothing, towels, boots, hair, and skin. Ultimately, it created in us a pride of unit and responsibility for one another lasting to this day.

Chapter 7

The First Haircut

Because we rarely encountered civilization, little things in the field became important. Not the least among the requirements was a regular haircut. The troop had a barber kit, manual clippers that could be used to give a relatively decent haircut. Haircuts would become particularly important if visitors were expected or if the hair finally got in the way of your helmet.

It was better to have short hair than long from a personal hygiene standpoint, particularly in the heat and humidity. After being in the field for about three weeks, especially after having short hair all my life, I needed a haircut.

We had several soldiers in the troop who could cut hair, but the normal barber was our Chieu Hoi. He was very good with the manual clippers and scissors and actually shaved with a straight razor around the ears. I knew all these facts, but once I sat down on the ammunition box that was his barber chair, and he put a towel around my neck, certain thoughts flashed in my mind.

The barber was a former NVA soldier. I was putting my life in his hands. Here was his chance to kill an American officer. Forget that he had not done anything to anyone else—this was my neck and his straight razor!

It was a silent haircut as I stiffly sat there. The Chieu Hoi went about his business, and I stiffened more as I heard him sharpening the razor on a strop. He carefully trimmed around the ears with the razor, then took a hold of my head. I was not ready for this as he quickly snapped my neck first left, then right, and gave a quick massage to my shoulders. The haircut was over, and I had survived it! Why hadn't anyone warned me about the neck snap? I guess the barber really was on our side.

More importantly, my neck actually felt good.

Chapter 8

Man on the Moon

We were not really very aware of what was happening in the news due to our relative isolation. We did get copies of the *Pacific Stars and Stripes* on an irregular basis if it was available when the resupply helicopter came out. The discontent at home really had little impact on us since we were too busy surviving the war, the daily grind, and the environment.

One thing that did capture everyone's imagination, however, was our race with the Soviets to the moon. Everyone in the platoon was at least an eight-year-old when the first Sputnik was launched and had lived through the early days of the Space Race in elementary and high school. We knew that Apollo 11, the first mission to land on the moon, had been launched and was on its way.

We were conducting a reconnaissance operation in the jungle northeast of Tay Ninh and were able to pick up Armed Forces Radio Vietnam. The morning had been quiet with no evidence of enemy activity.

We had paused for lunch, and the troopers were eating either C-rations (canned food) or Long Range Reconnaissance Patrol rations (dehydrated food pronounced "lurp" to which you added water to make it edible—and prized above C-rations). One of the track commanders, Sergeant Kurt Wolf, was really interested in the space program and had the Tay Ninh AFVN radio station tuned in.

"Listen up!" he yelled across the platoon position. We were all arrayed relatively close together in a fairly open area, catching what shade we could from nearby trees whiling eating lunch. "We're landing on the moon!"

Everyone stopped what he was doing and strained to hear the station. One of our soldiers had a thermometer on his vehicle. The temperature was 116 degrees Fahrenheit, and the sun was beating down. It was shortly after noon on July 20, 1969 (just after midnight on the American East Coast), as we heard the announcer from Mission Control in Houston, Texas describe the actions of astronaut Neil Armstrong.

When we heard Neil's words, "One small step for man, one giant leap for mankind," we all cheered. I don't think any American has forgotten where he or she was when we landed on the moon, and I am certain those soldiers in the platoon have not. We were proud of the United States and its space program achievements, even if we were at war sitting in the middle of a steamy jungle.

Chapter 9

Mobility

Because we were armored cavalry, we normally performed missions suited to our tracked mobility and firepower. We would dismount after we had driven through an enemy bunker complex or in the course of sweeping a road for mines. We didn't like to get off our tracks and normally would stay aboard, eating, sleeping, and performing other functions off the side.

One day in August while operating in heavy jungle, we came across evidence of enemy presence. There were numerous well-used trails and even some bloody bandages. We were, however, stopped from proceeding forward in our armored vehicles by a steeply banked stream. The only recourse was to cross the stream on foot with a reconnaissance patrol.

The Third Platoon was picked to conduct the patrol, and we selected five people to cross the stream and see what was on the other side. Meanwhile, another platoon sought to find a way across the stream in the vicinity. The remainder of the troop waited on the near side to react if necessary.

Those of us on the patrol quickly assembled and took extra ammunition for our M16s, a radio, and fragmentation and smoke grenades, then set off. As we surveyed the stream and went down the embankment, we discovered a hidden, low-slung footbridge that crossed the five-foot-wide stream. Our lead scout went across and turned left following a trail. I started across and had just set foot on the bridge when, from across the bridge to the right, appeared a North Vietnamese Army soldier wearing a light green pith helmet and carrying an AK-47.

We both looked at each other, startled. We both brought our weapons to bear at the same time and simultaneously pulled the triggers. Both weapons went "Click!" and failed to fire. As we both fell backwards off the bridge, the scout behind me carrying the radio shot the enemy soldier.

As we determined upon searching the enemy soldier, neither of us had a bullet chambered in our rifles, although both weapons were off safe with full magazines. Luckily, I had a scout following me who had his weapon ready with a round in the chamber. It always helps to conduct that one final check before starting off on foot.

The lead scout came running back at the sound of shots and was amazed he hadn't run into the enemy. I was just amazed at my dumb luck! I also learned to not be in such a hurry that you don't double-check the important things!

The situation heated up quickly, and I forgot about my luck. A fight started as the enemy bunker complex came alive. The platoon searching for a crossing had found one and began to work its way through the complex awaiting reinforcement by the rest of the troop. Our patrol scampered back to our tracks and moved to cross the stream following the path of the other vehicles.

The complex turned out to be a rather large affair, including an underground hospital. The troop swept the complex and stayed on site for two days, ferrying rice and other supplies out by cargo helicopter, crushing the bunkers with the weight of our vehicles and contaminating them with tear gas powder.

****

Later that same week we were given a new area of operations. The Nam Co and Saigon rivers bordered this new area in the infamous Iron Triangle. The Iron Triangle was a long-time enemy hideout within easy striking distance of Saigon. Our mission was to recon the area and see if any enemy activity was afoot. The area had been the scene of numerous earlier major battles. Because of its proximity to Saigon and to eliminate it as a hiding place, Agent Orange defoliants had denuded it and giant bulldozers called Rome plows cut down any remaining vegetation. The plows acted like giant jungle lawnmowers criss-crossing the jungle undergrowth, eliminating everything in their path. The resulting debris was then piled together, burned. Since the last Rome plow operation, elephant grass had grown over the area in some places to a height of eight to ten feet.

Consequently, as we drove our tracks through the elephant grass it was as if we were atop noisy rafts floating on a grass sea. All you could see were the tops of the ACAVs and Sheridans as we made our way. At the end of the day, to provide appropriate fields of fire and a landing area for resupply helicopters, the troop would perform giant wheeling maneuvers like aliens making crop circles, to knock down the grass.

The second day into the mission we were gliding on the sea when I looked to my left and watched a Sheridan simply disappear in a small cloud of dust. One minute it was there, and the next it was gone. I heard a garbled cry over the radio but could get no reply. I halted the platoon's sweep and maneuvered my track over to the dust cloud.

As we approached it became clear what had happened—the Sheridan had fallen upright into a giant pit or, more correctly, collapsed the top of a giant box. We weren't quite sure what it meant, but we sent for a tracked recovery vehicle from squadron. That vehicle, together with our own light recovery vehicle, managed to pull the Sheridan out of the pit.

The pit turned out to be a concrete-lined bunker. It was one of a series that contained hundreds of thousands of rounds of various type munitions, to include some dating back to the French Indochinese War in the late 1940s and early 1950s. We set up a perimeter around this find and began hauling out the prize. We stayed there the better part of three days pulling out cases of ammunition and other supplies. The more we found, the more there was.

Heavy lift cargo helicopters came in to transport the ammunition out, and all sorts of notables in the U.S. military came to visit the site. A reporting team from the *Stars and Stripes* newspaper even came out from Saigon to get the story. It was indeed a lucky find that fell into our laps, or rather, we fell into it.

Chapter 10

Monkeys, Dogs, the Bug Man, and Red Ants

As the troop continued its operations I continued to observe our environment.

American soldiers always try to make their surroundings homier and advance their interests, despite the environment. This trait was evident in the troop, even though our homes were very mobile.

The troop had a mascot, a small monkey that had somehow joined us prior to my arrival. The monkey, called Sarge, rode on the troop commander's track just like any of the crewmembers. He partook in the same rations as everyone else and slept on a small pad inside the track at night. Every once in a while he would disappear but never for very long. He knew he had a good deal and wasn't about to waste it.

He did, however, have one particularly nasty habit. In the course of a fight, with machineguns firing and loud explosions, he would masturbate. He would sit on the rear of his track with all the commotion going on around him and abuse himself. It was peculiar to be in battle and look over and watch this happen. When everything was over, Sarge would return to his normal ways.

Also in the troop was a dog named Pepe. The dog was a mixed breed and weighed no more than six pounds, if that. The dog was named after the skunk cartoon character, Pepe la Pew, and had been with the troop a long time. The dog and the monkey did not like each other, so the dog was parceled out to my platoon. He had apparently wandered into the troop while it was encamped in an old, deserted French fort along Route 13. He was handed down from one soldier to the next as their tours were finished. During a fight he would hide inside his track. He obviously had more sense than the monkey.

The dog, as did all Vietnamese dogs I observed, had a strange habit. Given a bone left over from one of our hot meals, he would bury it not with his paws but with his nose. He would find a soft spot of ground and use his nose to dig a hole. He actually was very efficient with this method. He then would cover up the hole by pushing the dirt back, again with his nose, and tamp it down. Never did I see a Vietnamese dog ever bury anything with its paws.

Since then I have always wondered whether dogs raised by Vietnamese in the U.S. do the same thing.

****

Although I was the only college graduate in my platoon, that did not mean the troops didn't have academic aspirations. Many had plans to go on to college under the GI Bill. In particular, there was one who wanted to become an entomologist.

I found this out one day as we were cleaning the debris off our tracks after a day's operation in the jungle. I approached one of the Sheridans and watched its driver, Marty Balzarini, very carefully sweeping around the splashboard on the front of his vehicle. The splashboard was made of plywood and could be rotated forward to become part of a barrier system designed to help the Sheridan float.

I asked him what he was doing. He explained that every day, he would collect all of the bugs that got smashed against or dropped onto his vehicle during the course of our travels. He would then pin them to the board on the front of his Sheridan and every evening would put them in plastic in his scrapbook, so he could send them home. In my head, I began calling him the bug man. The bug man explained, "I want to be an entomologist, and this place is full of specimens."

The bug man then proceeded to show me several books of catalogued insects with their names, and the date, time and approximate location where they were collected.

I often wonder what happened to the books and the bug man after he left Vietnam. I am sure that he loves the bug-obsessed forensic investigators on television.

****

The bug man aside, insects were often the bane of our existence. Once a week we choked down huge anti-malarial pills and, as night fell, carefully rolled down our sleeves and put on mosquito spray. Every track also had a supply of spray DDT in aerosol cans to counter insects. The buzz of mosquitoes often seemed to cause more sleepless nights than the enemy.

By far, however, the champion pest was the red ant. You could watch an individual ant crawl on you, find a bump or a patch of skin there, grab hold of it, and literally try to drag you off into his lair. These insects built tree nests that would often fall into our tracks as we passed through the jungle. When that happened, everything would stop while crewmembers frantically disrobed and slapped at the biting insects. We battled an enemy worse than the NVA with our aerosol cans. I have seen crews in the middle of a fight abandon the battle when they knocked a red ant nest into their track. With fire going on all around them, they would wage war against the red ant menace and not reenter the fight until this threat had first been eliminated.

Chapter 11

The Bunker

After six weeks in Vietnam and several firefights under my belt, I was feeling confident with the platoon. Several incidents brought home the point that we were involved in a dangerous business.

The first incident occurred as we came across an apparently deserted enemy bunker complex. On these occasions, the troop would set up a defensive perimeter and begin to search the bunkers for anything of value, particularly intelligence. It appeared that this complex had not been occupied for some time, and there was little in it of interest.

Each bunker had to be checked out, however, before it was destroyed or otherwise rendered uninhabitable. Teams were trained to do this methodically and carefully. Usually two or three soldiers would approach the entrance to the bunker, one tossing in a grenade to clear it while the others kept their weapons on the bunker before finally entering it themselves.

After a short time it became clear that there was no enemy in the complex. The kitchen bunker was empty with no sign of food or fire. The trails connecting the bunkers had not been used recently. As a matter of fact, the place was exceptionally clean.

With everything quiet I wandered off to check a bunker by myself. I lifted the cover to the entrance of a bunker and heard a small 'pfft' sound. In lifting the cover I had 'pulled the pin' on an enemy potato masher-style grenade. This weapon looks like the grenade you see the Nazis using in World War II movies, with a wooden handle for throwing and the explosive on the end of the handle. To arm the grenade, you pull a string on the end of the handle, and you have a few seconds to throw it before it explodes.

The cover on the bunker was attached to the grenade string while the grenade itself was anchored to the ground. When I pulled up the cover, it had yanked the string on the grenade and armed it. I realized what I had done, turned, and tried to run away!

I probably got no more than five feet when I tripped over a root on the jungle floor and fell to the ground. I lay there and a thousand things went through my head: should I get up and run, why are the buttons on my uniform so thick, do my jungle boots really have steel soles to protect my feet closest to the bunker, will the grenade go off, and is this really the way I want to die?

I could think of all these questions because time really seemed to slow down. My life did not flash before me, but snippets of time with my wife did, particularly how Kerry would kill me if she knew what had happened, interspersed in a blur with the questions I was asking myself. The time it took before the explosion was probably only two to three seconds but seemed a lifetime.

The grenade went off, and the noise was thunderous. Other than ringing in my ears, however, I was fine. The grenade had been placed just below ground level at the entrance to the bunker, but it was enough to spare me. The main force of the explosion had radiated upward. My clumsiness had saved my life. Upon the explosion, the troop alerted, but there was no firing. A scout came over and asked what happened.

I told him, and he laughed and then taught me a lesson that is a screen-saver on my computer even today: never pick up anything man-made on the battlefield! Regardless of whether it is a weapon or a piece of wood, if it looks man-made or man-emplaced, use a grappling hook to move it first, and you will avoid unpleasant surprises.

****

The second incident made clear the point that in war, a couple of inches can make all the difference.

We were in rather heavy contact with an enemy force that was defending their bunkers fiercely. The fight had begun at close distance, and the enemy seemed in no mood to retreat. The principal weapon on my track was a .50 caliber heavy machinegun, and I was firing it in bursts when suddenly it recoiled out of battery (jumped back not in the process of firing.) I performed what the army calls "immediate action" on the weapon, that is, pulling back on its charging handle and attempting to fire again. The gun resumed firing normally.

At the end of the fight, as we were sweeping the top of the track of expended brass and bullet links, I inspected my weapon. The machinegun had a flash suppressor attached to the end of its barrel. The cone of the flash suppressor bulged out on one side. Looking closer I discovered a squashed 7.62mm bullet (like those fired by an enemy AK-47) lodged between the end of the barrel and the attached flash suppressor. It was this bullet that caused the bulge and apparently caused my weapon to recoil strangely when the enemy bullet hit the end of the barrel.

Had the enemy firing the round aimed one or two inches differently, the flash suppressor would not have caught his round. The bullet might have traveled parallel to my .50 caliber barrel right at me. With the nonchalance of youth, I didn't think very much about it and tossed both the bullet and the damaged flash suppressor away. I now think I would like to have both the bullet and the flash suppressor back as a reminder that life is short.

Another incident about six weeks later made me wish I were not so nonchalant about throwing things away.

It occurred near the end of a large day-long battle involving most of the 1st Squadron in the rubber plantations near Loc Ninh, not far from the Cambodian border. As the fight was coming to a close, I saw three North Vietnamese soldiers running away across a road intersection. I maneuvered my track to investigate further when I heard the "thump-thump-thump" of mortars being fired. The enemy was either waiting for us to approach this intersection or had drawn us there. Whatever the plan was, it worked.

Just as we neared the intersection the enemy mortar rounds landed on the intersection where they had obviously been pre-planned. The explosions bracketed both the troop commander's and my own vehicle. It felt like someone had hit me on the back of my combat vehicle crewman's helmet (CVC—a fiberglass helmet with radio equipment fitted inside allowing the crew to communicate internally and externally through the vehicle radio) with a baseball bat. I flew forward, smashing my face into the back of my machinegun and knocking me out.

Big Al saw my track disappear in the explosions and assumed the worst, taking over the platoon. He tried to report my track's loss to the troop commander, who was also in the midst of these explosions.

After five minutes or so of unconsciousness, with my vehicle smoking, I rose out of the commander's hatch, fearing the worst.

There were killed and wounded on my track and I had blood pouring down my face. I knew I had been hit on the head and thought, "If you take your helmet off, your brains will spill out the back of your skull."

I very gingerly lifted my helmet off and patted the back of my head. There was no blood, but there were three large pieces of warm shrapnel in my longish hair, and three frayed, rooster tail-looking holes in the back of my helmet. Each piece of shrapnel was about the size of a fingertip up to the first joint. I combed the shrapnel out of my hair and threw it away and started to help the wounded on my track. I also made sure that the blood on my face was no more than a bloody nose.

****

Another strange thing happened earlier during this same battle.

The incident involved the troop commander, Captain Art West. In the course of the fight, the intensity of the action slowed, and he got off his track to coordinate plans with other leaders on the ground. As he did so, an enemy soldier sprang up armed with a pistol.

The two men faced one another as in a street gunfight in the Old West. The troop commander drew his .45 caliber pistol and began firing as the enemy fired his 9mm weapon. They could not have been more than 10-15 meters apart. Both were firing away as if they were on the streets of Dodge City. Neither was hit as the crews on the tracks around them sat stunned, watching the action. Finally, one of our machinegunners, probably more embarrassed by the fight and its results than anything, couldn't stand the suspense any more. He ripped off a short burst from his weapon and definitively ended the fight.

As always, after one of these incidents witnessed by the troopers, particularly one as strange as this, the story was told and retold and embellished in the troop of the gunfight at Dodge City.

****

The squadron later went on to win a Valorous Unit Citation for this battle. I have often wished I still had that CVC helmet and the three pieces of shrapnel. They would make interesting conversation pieces along with the bullet and my damaged flash suppressor. I also wished Big Al could have filmed the troop commander's gunfight.

Chapter 12

RPGs, Mines, Mortars, and Trees

While there were lots of ways of getting killed or injured in Vietnam, three direct and one indirect means were the most memorable.

Rocket-propelled grenades (RPGs) and land mines, the first direct means, put the fear of God in us every day. The enemy frequently used the RPG against us. The weapon was very accurate, especially at the short ranges our battles were fought. The Germans had developed the RPG in World War II, calling it the *panzerfaust*, to knock out armored vehicles. Because of its simplicity and ease of use, the Russians perfected it and then spread it throughout the world to become the favorite weapons of Third World armies. The RPG had a high explosive, anti-tank shaped charge warhead fired from a tube-like launcher by a rocket booster. It had a range of about two hundred meters. The weapon's shooter aimed and fired, leaving a big, white puffy back blast that looked like a giant cotton ball. A slow unguided rocket, you could literally watch it fly at you. If we saw an RPG being fired, we fired back with our machineguns just below the giant cotton ball. We could not affect the direction of the inbound rocket (because it had already been aimed), but we might get the shooter before the warhead arrived. At least, that was the theory, if you were fast enough!

We all hated the RPG because it could, with its shaped charge, burn a hole right through an ACAV and anything standing in the way. The RPGs we saw came in two models, the RPG-2 and the RPG-7, the latter having a better sight and consequently, more accuracy at a greater range. Normally many of our fights started with a volley of RPGs fired against us. Once, an RPG gunner rose up out of an irrigation ditch and fired an RPG at me while I looked around on the ground in a rubber plantation. It missed, going right over my head, bursting in the trees behind me. I can still recall the hot exhaust of the spent rocket on the back of my neck after it went by. The gunner turned and ran, exposing his RPG carrying vest to me with three ready RPG rounds stored in slots on his back. It did not take careful aim with my rifle to explode one of them.

Land mines, both manufactured and homemade, also caused great problems. Sometimes the enemy used our own dud artillery rounds rigged to explode, but normally we encountered a standard issue Chinese or Russian pressure mine. If you ran over the mine with your track, the pressure of the vehicle would be enough to set it off. Sometimes the enemy would get a little sophisticated and use a hydraulic device that would allow several vehicles to run over the mine before exploding. Sometimes the mines would be set to allow lightweight civilian traffic to pass over without incident, but when a heavy armored vehicle crossed its path, BOOM!

I only had one personal encounter with a mine in my time in Vietnam. My ACAV was down for maintenance and I commandeered a Sheridan. The first vehicle passed over the spot and then my track. There was a huge explosion with chunks of dirt and dust. As this happened, the Sheridan lurched up and then leaned to its right. I first thought that the track in front of me had hit a mine when I realized it was our vehicle. The entire right side of the Sheridan's suspension system, five sets of road wheels, disintegrated, and a big hole cratered the earth. The loss of all the suspension and the big hole caused the Sheridan to lean to the right into the void. Luckily, the explosion did not injure anyone, thanks to the armor plating that was installed on the belly of the track. The force of the explosion had blown the suspension system off and outward. Needless to say, the Sheridan had to go back to the United States for a complete rebuild.

****

Mortar attacks, the third direct means of attack, really didn't cause us much angst. Since we rarely stayed in the same spot two nights in a row, and we slept in our vehicles anyway, mortars did not cause us the anxiety that RPGs or mines did. The fixed camps of the Special Forces and the squadron headquarters fire base, where the squadron's artillery battery was also located, suffered much more from mortar attacks because of their fixed positions. The enemy rarely had the flexibility to target a cavalry troop on the move and didn't decide where to spend the night until just before the end of the day.

To drive home this point, during one operation we did come back to the same spot three nights in a row because of its handy location.

On the third night the enemy mortared us and never again, no matter what the lure of a known position, did we return to a site two nights in a row.

Another element, the weather, helped to negate the fear of mortar attack. We created a lot of mud with our tracked vehicles in the rainy season. The squadron headquarters position, especially, with a lot of tracks moving in and out of it, was usually a literal sea of mud. Once, as the platoon passed by, local enemy forces mortared the headquarters position. The only way you knew an attack had begun, however, was to carefully watch the enemy rounds hit, throw up a bucket of mud, followed by a loud "GLORP!" sound as they were swallowed up by the muddy sea, never to explode. I would imagine that there are still many places in Vietnam with a lot of shells six feet under waiting to cause trouble.

****

The final and indirect means involved the environment in which we operated. Thick foliage with large trees and heavy vines often marked the jungles of Vietnam. As we worked our way through the jungle, a track might entangle a vine in its treads, and begin to pull down the top of a tree. If the tree snapped off, it could well fall on a track and injure or even kill a trooper. Standard procedure had the crews watch out for one another and make sure that if the enemy didn't get you, a tree top wouldn't either. If your vehicle tangled with a vine, the unit would stop, pull out the machetes and axes, and the vehicle crew would cut themselves loose. Just another wonderful way to spend the day in the jungle!

The trees in a rubber plantation were also dangerous. While the rubber trees in the plantation had no vines to become entangled with, they were very fragile and one .50 caliber bullet through a tree could topple it onto a track, injuring (or worse) the crew riding on top. Needless to say, during a fight in the rubber, with .50 caliber bullets flying, you had to be careful a falling tree didn't get you as well.

****

Of course, you could always get shot in Vietnam from rifle or machinegun fire. That, however, was just another, common means of dying.

Every Track Had a Name Starting with a "C"

Photos of Platoon

Mr. Clean (Ron Mihalenko) on his Daily Routine.

Iron Ass (Mel Lafranchi) Taking in a Claymore Mine as Platoon Prepares to Leave the NDP.

Road Security Mission with a Convoy in the Background on Route 13 between Quan Loi and Saigon; Picture Taken Overlooking .50 Caliber Machinegun.

Man on the Moon Day, Sheltering in the Shade; ACAV in Foreground, Sheridan in Background

Most of the crews in Third Platoon: note their youth, and pick out the clean ones; see how the tracks, and soldiers all became the same color; Pepe is also shown; Big Al is second from right in picture at the left.

Chapter 13

Detritus

You could always tell where the 11th Cavalry had a battle. Unlike the light infantry units in Vietnam that were restricted by what they could carry on their backs, we had the luxury of carrying "extras."

Our Mermite cans have already been discussed. Indeed, our crews considered them not a luxury but necessities, despite the fact that infantry units did without. We also carried cases of soda and extra C-ration meals aboard our tracks, for use if daily resupply could not reach us due to weather or our location.

We had plastic water bowls with which to shave and clean up instead of having to use our helmets. We carried five-gallon cans of water, both for us and for the track's radiator cooling system. We also carried folding lawn chairs that we purchased from the local populace to sit behind our tracks in our night defensive positions. They were always stowed at evening stand-to.

Indeed, the lawn chair marked a cavalry battlefield. When a fight would start, invariably some of the track crews would throw the folding chairs over the side hurrying to get at their ammunition to reload their weapons. At other times, when the crews needed room to aim their weapons, they ditched overboard the chairs stowed folded and piled neatly on top of the tracks. In either event, as we maneuvered we ran over the chairs—or simply left them behind as the battle progressed.

Consequently, a cavalry battleground had distinctive characteristics. You would find the normal spent brass shell casings from the machineguns, crushed olive drab ammunition cans, and black expended machinegun bullet links. However, you would also find green Wink and red Coke cans and mangled aluminum folding lawn chairs. Surely the locals ultimately scavenged our battlefields, repaired the chairs, and resold them to us. Unfortunately, due to our pace of operations, we had a high demand for new chairs.

Chapter 14

Strange Occurrences

I have indicated that most of our fights took place at very close range, with little time to react. We might lose the first ten seconds of a battle, but our overwhelming firepower would be soon brought to bear, and essentially the fight shortly ended. We also worked in what were essentially "free fire" zones, so, if we were engaged, we could shoot back with few worries about collateral damage or civilian casualties.

During the course of one such fight in October, the platoon's line of tracks moved through a complex when suddenly, directly in front of my track—literally two feet in front— up popped an enemy soldier out of his hiding place, a spider hole entry to an underground tunnel complex. The track driver did not see him, because he was so close, nor could I depress my machinegun enough to fire at him. I yelled at my side machinegunners to do something, but they could not hear me over the battle noise, nor could they see him because of his location directly to my front.

The enemy soldier then proceeded to climb hand over hand right up the front slope of the track. I grabbed for my M16 beside me to bring it to bear. The driver finally saw the soldier, but we were both too surprised and dumbfounded by the enemy's bravery and skill to react quickly. He kept climbing and arrived on top of the track, right in my face, screaming, "Chieu hoi! Chieu hoi!" He was surrendering!

We got credit for a prisoner, but we took a terrible ribbing from the platoon for allowing this guy to board our track right under our noses without anyone taking any action. I made sure from then on my driver a pistol at the ready. I also practiced pulling the rear-locking pin quickly out of the .50 caliber machinegun mount, so it would fire directly down the front slope of the track.

Later in my army career, I designed a scenario on a live-fire range that required both the driver and the track commander to react to a similar situation.

****

Also about this time, when I had several months experience under my belt as a platoon leader, a most unusual occurrence happened. I have seen this situation depicted only once in any war movie. In the film, *Saving Private Ryan*, Tom Hanks disembarks his landing craft and makes his way up the beach. At one point in this scene he shelters behind a German obstacle, and all the sound of battle around him stops. He looks around but doesn't hear a thing, perhaps overwhelmed by the violence.

The same thing happened to me, with an added component. The platoon got into a fight in the rubber, when, suddenly, I found the battlefield silent despite all the gunfire. Not only was it silent, but everything happening around me occurred in slow motion. I still gave orders and used my weapon, but all other action seemed to slow down in time. During this eerie situation I also felt supernaturally efficient. I could do my job in normal time while everyone else moved so slowly. I had a heightened ability to observe the battlefield, pick out targets, and make decisions. I could even see the individual machinegun bullets leaving my weapon. The feeling lasted for several minutes when, just as quickly, I snapped back into real time, and the noise erupted.

This feeling never happened to me again during my tour, but if it could be captured, it would add tremendously to our fighting capability.

Chapter 15

Sheridans

All our tracks became like members of the family. Each seemed to have certain innate and individual characteristics, almost their own personalities. I could always count on one track to break its torsion bars (the armored vehicle equivalent of shock absorbers) while another would go through road wheel hubs with great regularity. One track always had radio problems. The Sheridan, though, had its own peculiar issues and other problems.

Our Sheridans were idiosyncratic vehicles and high-tech for the time. They were essentially light tanks—the army officially called the Sheridan an "Armored Reconnaissance Airborne Assault Vehicle" (or ARAAV, pronounced "a-rav")—with an all-electrical turret and a huge main gun designed to fire both conventional tank rounds or launch anti-tank missiles. In Vietnam we carried no missiles or associated equipment and fired principally conventional anti-personnel rounds, called "canister." This ammunition acted like shotgun shells, exploding ten thousand flechettes (small one and one-half inch long darts) at the enemy, literally shredding the jungle and everything else in its path out to a distance of one hundred meters or more.

Another technological feature of the vehicle included main gun cartridge cases that burned when the gun fired, leaving no conventional shell casing. The Sheridan's system would then blow compressed air down the gun tube to eliminate any burning residue before the loader loaded a new round. Between the compressed air, the tropical climate's effects on its electrical turret, and cartridge cases that would swell in the humidity, Sheridans often gave us fits, and its crewmen used ingenious means to keep them operational.

The speedy Sheridan could easily keep up with a wheeled supply convoy. On Route 13 these convoys did not waste time, but I have observed a Sheridan pass with ease a line of trucks that were going at least 50 miles per hour.

On one occasion an RPG hit a platoon Sheridan and penetrated its outer metal skin. The vehicle really had little armored protection—a thin metal outer skin, behind it a foam layer (the Sheridan had an amphibious capability), followed by light aluminum armor. The RPG round stuck in the foam and did not explode. The round, however, hit the Sheridan at 90 degrees pointing right at the driver's compartment. When the fighting stopped, the crew began cleaning their vehicle when they found the RPG sticking out of the side of their vehicle like an arrow. The crew immediately called Big Al and me over. "What are we going to do?" they asked.

We couldn't very well let them ride around in the vehicle and take the chance the RPG would explode, surely killing the driver. We had to remove it, and we couldn't wait for an explosive ordnance demolition technician to come out to the field.

We got out our tools: can openers to widen the hole in the outer skin, pliers to pull back the skin, spoons to dig out the foam, and communications wire to wrap around the rocket part of the grenade to pull the warhead out of the vehicle. All the while we worked very gingerly, not wanting to cause the round to go off and damage the vehicle or kill us.

Finally, the grenade had been nearly exposed. We wrapped the wire around it and moved back a considerable distance. Grabbing several pairs of gloves, four of us yanked on the wire and fell to the ground. Unbelievably, the wire had snapped. We walked up to the Sheridan, looking at the grenade still sticking out. We repeated this maneuver three more times without success. Each time we did this we feared causing the grenade to become more sensitive.

Big Al and I huddled. We had to move, and the current course of action didn't work. The demolitions man in the platoon, Earl Sizemore, said mischievously he had never blown up a Sheridan before but would sure like to give it a try. We decided to let him do his thing. We unloaded everything of value from the Sheridan, to include its ammunition.

The demo man packed a small amount of C-4 plastic explosive around the RPG, telling us he hoped this technique would blow the round apart before the RPG exploded and destroyed the Sheridan. We backed off and lit the time fuse.

The C-4 detonated with a minor explosion. We ran back to discover the RPG's shaped charge had in fact been detonated by the C-4 and put a hole in the Sheridan. Our plan had not worked. The Sheridan would have to be returned to a stateside depot for rebuild. The RPG had ultimately, if belatedly, done its work, though thankfully without any loss of life.

The demo man later painted a Sheridan outline on the side of his track, *Clarence*, slyly marking his dubious achievement.

****

Another Sheridan incident related to this one also did not result in the loss of life. It surely scared the hell out of a lot of infantrymen, however.

The crew of the damaged Sheridan ultimately drove their vehicle back to the troop's rear and picked up a new Sheridan. They transferred their gear, weapons, and ammunition from the old track to the new and prepared to return to the field. The night before they were scheduled to rejoin us, some 1st Cavalry Division infantrymen at an enlisted club in Quan Loi apparently insulted one of the Sheridan crewmembers. Being a good 11th Cavalry trooper, he did not take insults lightly.

Instead, he went to the track park and got in his Sheridan and drove it over to the club. He knocked in the door of the club with the Sheridan's gun tube and fired a giant whoosh of compressed air. The club emptied with a lot of infantrymen soiling themselves. It also confirms the thoughts of many in the army that the Cavalry knows when to use hot air.

Thankfully the troop executive officer, Rick Wagner, got the Sheridan and its crew out the gate early the next morning before the military police showed up. The crew waited down the road from the gate until the platoon rendezvoused with the Sheridan a couple of hours later. Off we went on our new mission, never hearing anything about the incident again.

Chapter 16

Donut Dollies and Chaplains

On one occasion during the middle of a sweep in the jungle we were told over the radio to assemble the troop in a big jungle clearing, circling the wagons because important visitors were arriving. Moreover, we were to clean up and, if we had clean uniforms, put them on with the proper rank.

About an hour later we were set, and a Huey helicopter from regiment flew over. We popped smoke to give the pilot wind direction, and he did a 180-degree turn. He landed in the middle of our position, and out of the helicopter climbed two American Red Cross donut dollies (donut dollies date back to World War I when the Red Cross used volunteers to hand out donuts to the troops.) They had with them bags of goodies including writing paper and envelopes, paperback books, decks of cards, and candy. They also had games.

They were dressed in their light blue Red Cross cotton shifts and were wearing floppy boonie hats to ward off the sun. To eyes starved for American girls, they looked gorgeous. They were probably in their mid- to late-twenties. They laughed and smiled and made us happy and seemed oblivious to being in a war zone.

The dollies split up, each going to a platoon on the perimeter. While the tracks left one man aboard for perimeter security, the rest of the platoon gathered around the girl. If she felt ill at ease, we certainly didn't know. She played get-to-know-you games, like *Game of the States*, asking members of the platoon where they came from and sticking outlines of the states on a board. Not surprisingly, most members of the platoon came either from the south or mid-west. Fewer soldiers came from the east or west coasts. When she had completed the row of states across the southern U.S. border, she gave the last trooper to respond a box of cookies, and everyone cheered. Like a kindergarten class we played *Pin the Tail on the Donkey* and

Battleship. The platoon acted like silly boys in front of the donut dolly when just moments before her arrival they had considered themselves hardened soldiers.

After about thirty minutes with us she went on to another platoon. We looked about at each other sheepishly, but each of us cherished the time with someone from the outside world. The two women helicoptered out to another troop after about ninety minutes with us. We went back to war.

****

The chaplains from regiment would also visit intermittently. Anytime they landed it became Sunday. The same protocol for welcoming the donut dollies worked for the chaplains, except we didn't have to clean up. The chaplains also brought goodies, usually writing paper and envelopes, plus small copies of the New Testament.

The Catholics would gather around a makeshift altar to attend Mass. There were usually eight to ten soldiers in the 'congregation.' Iron Ass, an Italian-American Catholic, especially given his experience, always attended. The other Protestant denominations would hold their service at the same time.

The priest would hear confessions before Mass and give us a burst of the glory gun in his short sermon. There normally would be no singing, and the visit would be wrapped up in less than 30 minutes before the chaplains dropped in on another unit. Sometimes the chaplains had to be denied landing permission, because operational necessities demanded it. After attending Mass, I would always feel at peace with our situation.

It is said there are no atheists in a foxhole, and it seemed we had few in the platoon. Once, after the loss of a soldier from Tennessee, the platoon put its money together to buy an illustrated Bible to send to the soldier's family. We inscribed the Bible and dedicated it to the lost soldier and his family. Everyone from the platoon signed the Bible's inside front cover. I hope that act and the Bible consoled the family.

Chapter 17

Others

We did not spend every night in the jungle. Sometimes when we were on road security missions, we would stay on or near the road itself.

Most of our road security missions involved Route 13, an important supply route that led north from Saigon to the Cambodian border. The road passed close to enemy base areas and had been and would be the site of several major battles.

Spotted along Route 13 were active and abandoned firebases. Artillery batteries would position themselves there to support ground operations taking place within range of their weapons. Some of these bases had not been used in recent memory but seemed to be good locations for units to remain overnight.

Once, after relief from a road security mission, Charlie Troop's platoons and the troop headquarters all assembled at one of these bases for resupply in preparation for heading off on a new mission the next day. We pulled in behind the firebase's abandoned berm and performed our normal tasks getting ready for the night.

Darkness fell, and I went to sleep around ten PM fully clothed as usual, intending to get up around midnight to walk the perimeter. I had been asleep in the track for perhaps an hour with the two other off-duty crewmembers when I had the distinct feeling there were others present. I felt tiny claws walking up my chest. I opened my eyes and found myself staring at the beady eyes of a rat!

I yelped and alerted the other two crewmembers inside the track. We leapt up and warned the rest of the troop. Several other tracks already had become aware of the problem. Apparently the rats came out of hiding after dark and somehow scurried from the firebase's berm onto our vehicles. We beat a hasty night retreat from that firebase, reminiscent of the retreat after the tear gas attack, only this time defeated by monster rats. The troop moved off about five hundred meters and set up a hasty linear position astride the road itself. We doubled our security while we made sure the rats were gone. Needless to say, we were happy to see dawn come without further incident.

A couple of days later one track found a rat still aboard, and Pepe the dog chased it off. Pepe had finally earned his keep.

Chapter 18

Flying with the Air Force

The regiment had a program in which armored cavalry platoon leaders traded places with Air Force pilots for what amounted to a long weekend. Each service member could experience the other's day-to-day duties and learn more about the other service. Needless to say, what a deal for the army guy!

In the fall of 1969 the squadron selected me for the program. I waited for the incoming resupply helicopter that was ferrying out the exchange pilot. He flew the two-seat A-37 Dragonfly, a small twin-jet attack aircraft that could carry bombs and rockets, in a fighter squadron assigned to Bien Hoa Air Base. The Air Force used this airplane into the 21st Century as a pilot training aircraft.

I met the pilot as he got on the ground and introduced him to Big Al. Evening was coming, and the troop's mortars prepared to fire illumination rounds while we completed resupply.

The Air Force pilot was obviously uncomfortable on the ground, especially in the middle of the jungle as it grew dark. A mortar tube fired its illumination round without warning, and he looked around anxiously for a rock to hide under. We assured him the mortar round was outgoing and not incoming. I told him to enjoy himself, and that Big Al would take good care of him. He said, "Thanks," but did not look too confident.

With resupply complete, I got aboard the helicopter. I said goodbye to Big Al and the pilot and left for Blackhorse base camp where I would be ferried over the Bien Hoa Air Base and join an Air Force fighter-bomber squadron for a couple of days.

I must have appeared somewhat scruffy when I showed up at Bien Hoa, but I felt heartily welcomed by the Air Force anyway. The flying squadron's operations officer explained the schedule for the next day, what training I would have to undergo before I flew on a mission, and then we ate at the squadron dining hall. He then pointed out my sleeping accommodations, and I knew then, between the mess hall and the bed with real sheets, I had landed in a different world.

The next morning after breakfast, the pre-flight training began. After a squadron overview briefing (the most important point being that the squadron had never lost an airplane since it had arrived three years earlier in Vietnam), an Air Force technician explained the survival gear and how it functioned, the types of missions the squadron flew, and what ordnance was used. Finally, he also checked me out in the ejection seat trainer and told me how to prevent blood from flowing away from the brain while the aircraft maneuvered. Since we did not wear G-suits, the tech advised me to tighten my stomach and thigh muscles to keep blood from pooling in my lower extremities.

The mission pilot and I walked out to his aircraft for a cockpit familiarization. The pilot kept that part of the training army simple. He pointed out all the dials, gauges, and switches, the rudder pedals, and the stick and said simply, "Don't touch anything!" I couldn't have agreed more.

I also had the opportunity to address the squadron's pilots on the life of a platoon leader on the ground. I gave them the description of a day on the ground and our equipment, and the importance we placed on timely air support. I'm sure that my description probably bore little resemblance to what my pilot counterpart said to his mates when he got back. I knew my description of life with the Air Force squadron would not be believed back at the platoon.

Finally the time came to fly. I suited up and received a flight helmet. After the mission briefing, we did the walk-around of the airplane and started engines. The mission ordered us to fly on-call air support of ground troops in contact in the III Corps Tactical Zone (basically the area around Saigon and north to the Cambodian border.) If a unit needed our help, we would be dispatched to its assistance and given further instructions by an Air Force Forward Air Controller or FAC on site. My impression of the take off was one of immense speed, for I had been in the jungle for months going at a snail's pace.

The airplane's cockpit was very hot initially but cooled once we got to altitude. We joined in a two-ship flight and kept in a racetrack pattern north of Saigon awaiting a call. It didn't take very long for that to occur.

A 1st Infantry Division mechanized unit was in contact west of Route 13. I found it amazing to look down at the earth and broadly recognize places that were intimately familiar to me. We went to the location of the call and contacted the FAC while flying in a holding pattern above the battle. The only indication of a fight on the ground was one small explosion; otherwise, everything appeared quiet. The FAC rolled in and fired white phosphorous rockets to mark where he wanted us to bomb.

The pilot confirmed his run-in line and the target, and off we went. I don't know how far above the ground we were when we dropped the first bomb, but I do know the dive seemed steep and the pull out strained me more than I expected. I did as I had been trained and tightened my thighs and stomach. Unfortunately, I don't think I remembered to unclench the muscles until the mission finished. We made several more passes until we were out of ordnance and returned to base.

We flew a similar mission that afternoon and the next morning, and then it was time for me to return to the platoon. I was exhausted after each flight, literally drenched in sweat and with a queasy stomach. It may have had something to do with keeping my muscles tightened, but more likely the physical intensity of the flights just tired me out. The pilots had to be sharp and in good condition.

I experienced, however, a great difference between ground and air operations. From the air, despite the strenuousness, exactitude, and professionalism of the flying, events on the ground appeared noiseless, distant, and, I can't think of a better word, antiseptic—no yelling, no noise of explosions and gunfire, no dust or debris, and no blood.

****

This story has an epilogue. My youngest child, Sean, graduated from the Air Force Academy, took his pilot training on the T-37 Tweet (the training version of the A-37) 31 years after my escapade, and currently flies an A-10 Warthog pilot. The A-10's mission is to support ground troops and go after enemy tanks in particular. I wonder if this is the Air Force's way of getting back at me.

****

I had other encounters with the Air Force. A couple, in particular, showed the power the Air Force had at its disposal. We would sometimes conduct BDA (bomb damage assessment) missions after B-52 heavy bombers would carpet bomb a suspected enemy concentration or base area within our area of operations. For our own safety, we maintained a distance no closer than three thousand meters (almost two miles) from the target area (a swath a couple of kilometer wide by several long), awaiting the bombing's completion, then drove into the area to see what was to be found.

Usually we found very little in the target area for it looked like the surface of the moon: huge bomb craters already filling with water, defoliated landscape, and scarred tree trunks tossed on their sides, roots and all. Usually a complete quiet overcame the area because any wildlife that had been there was gone, in one way or another. However, sometimes one could escape this destruction. Once we came across three NVA soldiers bathing in a new bomb crater. They probably couldn't hear us coming because they had been deafened by the bomb blasts, and they didn't last very long.

****

Normally our air support consisted of an OV-10 Bronco Forward Air Controller (FAC) observation plane that had two propellers and looked very odd. One propeller was in front of the pilot and pulled the plane while the other was behind the pilot and pushed it. Hence the light plane had a "pull-me, push-you" system and marked enemy targets with white phosphorous rockets.

The FAC would be assigned an area and assist troops on the ground by calling in fast movers, usually in our case, two F-4 Phantom jets or two A-37s. We often urged the pilot, if nothing was going on, to give us an "air show." He would oblige with barrel rolls and low passes, then go about his business. Once, after taking small arms fire from a clump of jungle near the Cambodian border, the FAC ordered some fighters to bomb the area. We withdrew some 500 meters and got down inside our tracks. In came the F-4s to drop 750-pound "hi-drag" bombs. The jets would focus on the FAC's white phosphorous marking rounds and make a fast, low approach across our front dropping their bombs. The low approach improved accuracy but required that the bombs be retarded after they were released, so they wouldn't blow up the airplanes above. Hence, the bombs had high-drag fins on them that popped out and slowed the bombs after they dropped, given the releasing aircraft time to get away.

The planes made two passes each, dropping two bombs each time. Even though we were far away half a kilometer away, the thunderous explosions shook us inside our tracks. Once the jets finished their mission, we approached the area. Five minutes later the heavens opened up, and it rained mud on us from all the dirt in the air coupled with the rainstorm.

I wonder if the jets caused the rainstorm. They did take care of the enemy small arms fire.

Chapter 19

Rome Plows, Rockets, and Helicopter Pilots

The Rome plows that enabled the earlier incident in the Iron Triangle when a Sheridan collapsed a bunker were very welcome assets on Route 13 when the troop pulled road and convoy security missions. A Rome plow company's mission along Route 13 called for it to plow back the jungle up to one hundred meters from the side of the main road, pile up all the resulting debris, and burn it. It would not take the jungle long to recover, but in the meanwhile, the plows made units and convoys using the road safer from a close-in ambush.

An added benefit of the plowing, at least to armored units, meant the possibility of not using the road at all, thereby avoiding the danger of mines. Since our Rome plow brethren had mowed down the jungle, we could make our own roads adjacent to the main road by simply wearing down the remaining jungle growth. We found these roads almost as fast as using the main road itself. Mind you, rarely did we travel faster than ten to fifteen miles per hour.

****

Once, while on a road security mission, I got an urgent message from a light helicopter pilot who was providing security over the convoy and scouting ahead. He claimed to have sighted a 122mm rocket on stakes aimed at the convoy's route. Moreover, the rocket had a trail of smoke coming from its rear! He needed somebody on the ground to race over there and investigate—to prevent catastrophe.

As the closest to the coordinates he gave us, my track cranked up and went over to the spot, about a mile away. The pilot hovered over the site about fifteen feet in the air, making the rocket easy to find on a small bare hill about 25 yards off the road. As we approached the spot, we started looking around for enemy activity. The Rome plows had done a pretty good job here, with just scattered limbs and brush around.

We called on the radio to the pilot and said we didn't see anything. The pilot was adamant—the rocket was right there! We told him to hover away, dismounted the track, and went over to the spot. He indicated we were there. We saw a small tree trunk about five feet long, four inches in diameter that had been burned. The rocket certainly resembled a tree.

Two things happened here. First, what happens on the ground is always different than it looks like from the air, even at fifteen feet altitude. Second, the helicopter pilot probably went back to base and told all his buddies that he found a rocket, but the stupid armored cavalry walked right over it and couldn't see it. Likely he also made a remark to the effect that they couldn't find their own ass with both hands.

It doesn't take much altitude to cause a difference between those who fight in the air and those guys on the ground.

****

I have seen helicopter pilots, however, do amazing things with great regularity and skill. Medevac (radio call sign "dust-off") pilots often would were courageously land under fire, often just behind the line of troops in contact with the enemy. Once, in that very situation, the dust-off helicopter came in with its side doors open to pick up our wounded. No sooner had he landed than an RPG fired at our tracks passed through our lines, in and out of the helicopter through its open doors, only to explode in the jungle on the far side. The helicopter crew kept taking care of the wounded and took off without another thought. I am sure there were a couple of stories told later that night when the crew went off duty.

I also have a lot of respect for the heavy lift helicopter pilots that kept us resupplied every night. They would often hover their helicopters with heavy sling loads underneath into small landing zones that we had hacked out of the jungle. More than once I saw the Chinook hover into a hole in the jungle barely large enough for the helicopter's dual rotors to fit. They took blade strikes from the foliage, too, as they lifted off, with very tight clearances.

During the latter half of my tour, I did witness some gamesmanship between two heavy lift helicopters. One of our tracks had been so badly damaged it could not be towed out of the jungle to be repaired at a base camp. We arranged for a new model Chinook (with an increased lift capacity) to come in and lift the track out. Before the helicopter came, however, we emptied it of all its fuel, its armored belly plate, its tracks, and all interior supplies to make it as light as possible. We attached the lift cables, and in came the helicopter as advertised. The pilot knew absolutely his brand new toy could do the job.

Just like the wolf in the fairy tale, though he huffed and puffed, he couldn't seem to lift the damaged track off the ground. He tried a number of times and became concerned that he would break his helicopter (perhaps the track's suction just kept it stuck in the mud!).

As his tribulations continued, a passing CH-54 Skycrane heavy lift helicopter passed by. This crew decided to get into the fray and offered to help. The Chinook crew gave up, and we accepted Skycrane's invitation. The new crew swooped down and, much to the chagrin of the Chinook crew picked the track up and carried it off for repair.

Again, I'm certain that the Skycrane's crew spent a good part of that evening regaling their fellows about the adventure and the impotence of the Chinook.

Chapter 20

Thunder Run

Thunder Run is a term used generally to describe a high-speed military column that uses offensive tactics and heavy weaponry to keep the enemy at bay along a dangerous stretch of road. The 11th Cavalry would often use such a tactic to clear a route ahead of a ground resupply convoy. A column of Sheridans, tanks, and ACAVs rumbling down a road firing their weapons to suppress anything alongside the road makes one proud to be in Armor.

In early November, the platoon split into two sections to overwatch a section of road on which there had been frequent enemy mining activity. I positioned the sections more than a kilometer apart, so we could still watch the road but not mistakenly shoot each other.

A call from troop headquarters came around midnight. The troop commander told me to quickly assemble the platoon and report about twenty kilometers away to help defend a provincial capital town. A reported force of five hundred North Vietnamese army soldiers threatened an imminent attack. "Oh, and by the way," the radio said, "did you know that the enemy force is between you and the town?"

Big Al had in charge of the other section, so when we had reassembled on the road, we got together to discuss the situation and then brief the track commanders. We decided that since we would not be passing through any villages on the way to our destination, we would conduct a Thunder Run down the road to the town. The Thunder Run would start about ten kilometers out from the town.

After briefing everyone in the platoon on the danger of the enemy situation, we reviewed the signals to start and cease firing and everyone's responsibility for our moving fields of fire. We covered what light discipline we would use, what to do in case of casualties, and how to array the platoon for the defense of the town, if and when we managed to get there safely.

The night was cloudless and black with only the stars that shown so brightly at night in Vietnam. We started out slowly with everyone alert at his weapon and munitions ready for use. The ACAV's fifth crewman, if one was available, prepared to add to the offensive show with his grenade launcher.

We had not gone very far when a torrential rain started. The wind whipped us, but no one donned any raingear. As we approached the intersection where we had decided to begin the Thunder Run, I had my driver flip on the track's headlights (not all lights in the platoon worked because they were often damaged during operations). The show started as we picked up speed.

Machinegun fire erupted left and right from the column of tracks. We threw trip flares over the side as well as hand grenades. The fifth crewman fired 40mm grenades from his grenade launcher. We popped parachute flares in the air, and generally created as much havoc as possible whether we saw anything or not. We received no return fire, and the road was clear. We also began to call for artillery illumination rounds to help us as we approached the link up with the rest of the troop.

About a kilometer out of town we slowed a bit and ceased fire with the heavy weaponry. We fired only our M16 rifles over the side. Shortly thereafter we ceased fire entirely and passed through the troop checkpoint and made our way to the section of the town's perimeter we were to defend. The rain finally let up.

After checking on our initial dispositions, I reported to the troop commander. It was almost three AM, and the adrenalin still pumped. I told him we had seen nothing on the way in. He welcomed me and congratulated the platoon for arriving in good shape. As he was talking, a call came in from squadron saying the report of a five hundred-man enemy force was a false alarm. For now, the squadron ordered us to defend the town and prepare for other operations; instructions would be sent to us in the morning. Thank you very much.

I went back to the platoon and had the troops revert to normal security posture. With all the excitement of the night, however, I'm sure no one slept, and dawn found us a fatigued unit, with the adrenalin boost gone and no sleep.

****

My eldest child, Megan, was commissioned an officer in army Military Intelligence after her graduation from West Point. I hope she went into that branch to prevent any more false alarms.

Chapter 21

Thanksgiving

The army always makes Thanksgiving a big day for troops in the field. The cooks pull out all the stops, and the logisticians do us proud. The platoon was again pulling a road security mission early in the day and planned to reassemble with the troop that afternoon to prepare for the big Thanksgiving meal that would be sent out to us.

Just as the resupply helicopter was landing, however, the platoon was alerted to mount up and clear a stretch of road that led from War Zone D, up near the Cambodian border, checking it for mines. The 3rd Squadron had been operating in the area for a couple of weeks and had gotten in several big fights and now was going to use the road to regroup. Part of 3rd Squadron was coming out on a road that it had not expected to use, and it had to be cleared.

The platoon looked wistfully at the Mermite cans filled with turkey and all the trimmings as we moved out. We divided the road into two stretches, and half the platoon swept one stretch while the other half leap-frogged ahead parallel to the road to begin sweeping its section of the road.

A road sweep is a very meticulous task involving teams of soldiers with hand-held minesweepers covering every square foot of the road and marking suspicious areas. Meanwhile, the tracks overwatch the teams on the ground, the left and right of the road, plus the ground already covered.

The schedule called for the 3rd Squadron to leave War Zone D at six PM, so we only had about three hours for each half of the platoon to sweep about five kilometers of road. My half of the platoon took the stretch closest to War Zone D and worked its way toward a stream-crossing site, our linkup with 3rd Squadron elements.

We made the linkup point having found only a couple of suspicious areas where the minesweepers beeped. Since we had no time to spare, the demolition man came forward while the minesweeping team pushed ahead out of blast danger. He set a small charge on the area in question, and we blew it up. Neither area indicated afterwards any evidence of mining. Big Al reported his area clear then moved to join us at the crossing site.

Three company-sized units of the 3rd Squadron came across the stream over an armored vehicle launched bridge. They looked like a weary Macy's Thanksgiving Day Parade without the giant balloons and marching bands. You could see some of the vehicles had RPG holes and shrapnel spray on their sides, and the soldiers looked tired.

It took about ninety minutes to get them across and up the road to their assembly areas. When the bridge recovered, we mounted up and returned up the same road to the position we had left earlier that afternoon. We were the last platoon to recover about two hours after dark with Thanksgiving Day pretty much shot.

Everyone did manage to get some cold turkey and a piece of pumpkin pie—still a Thanksgiving feast but without all the trimmings. At least we had helped 3rd Squadron.

Chapter 22

Ambush

When we were out in the jungle, in addition to our defensive perimeter preparations, we would often conduct dismounted ambush patrols. These patrols would position themselves on likely foot approaches to the troop's position, often on trails we had seen during the day.

The platoon leader usually led these patrols. His platoon sergeant would lead a mounted reaction force if the patrol got into trouble. Detailed standard operating procedures guided all the preparations for the patrol. Our patrols usually consisted of six men in two three-man groups. No one going on the patrol had bathed recently, so no enemy could pick up a clean scent. Each group had an M60 machinegun. All three men in the group carried ammunition for it. Each man also had his own rifle with extra ammunition plus several hand grenades, trip flares, and Claymore mines. One man in the patrol carried a radio for communication back to the troop headquarters. Everyone carried water and the usual first aid packs. The troop's mortars preplanned fires around the patrol's position and linkup signals and challenge and password were set. The patrol leader selected a route to and a different return route from the ambush site.

After evening chow (the patrol's members were first to eat), the patrol leader held a final patrol briefing and equipment check. The patrol then left the perimeter, and troop sealed the perimeter behind it. The patrol made its way to the ambush site at twilight, usually eight hundred to one thousand meters away. On the way into the ambush site I indicated a designated rallying point to everyone in the patrol should the patrol have to abandon its primary position and assemble there.

Once at the chosen site, the two groups split up and settled into their positions twenty to forty meters apart, setting up firing stakes delineating fields of fire that would cross in the selected kill zone.

Each group then proceeded to lay down their rain ponchos on the ground and begin other preparations. Each group linked its entire supply of machinegun ammunition together, and then daisy-chained its Claymore mines, so they would all go off in the kill zone with one click of the detonator. Lastly each group emplaced its trip flares. Assembling at the group position, we prepared and laid out our hand grenades on the ponchos.

We strung communications wire between the two groups. The wire linked one group with the other group that had the radio. A series of distinct pulls on the wire provided silent information between the groups, e.g., one pull—"You OK?" two pulls in return—"OK." Three distinct pulls in succession meant awaken everyone, something's up. Four sharp pulls meant we would execute the ambush when the flares went off and then move immediately to the rally point.

The first part of the night passed quietly. Each group formed a human sandwich, lying side-by-side with two riflemen on the outside and the machinegunner in the middle. One man in each group remained awake and had the wire tied around his wrist. We maintained communications with troop headquarters every half hour by "breaking squelch" on the radio (squeezing the radio's handset twice in response to a whispered call for status). The two squeezes indicated everything was all right. The jungle made its usual noises on this moonless night.

"I hear something," said my machinegunner who was on alert as he nudged me awake. I listened closely, but could hear nothing but the usual jungle background noise. Gradually another noise grew. I alerted the other group with three pulls of the wire, followed by their two pulls in return, as they indicated their readiness.

The noise got louder coming down the trail. I swear to this day it sounded like the Wicked Witch of the West's army on their trek to capture Dorothy and Toto in the *Wizard of Oz*. The enemy soldiers marched in seeming cadence right down the trail, making this unworldly sound.

I decided we had no choice—I carefully yanked the wire four times, and we got ready for the trip flares to ignite.

We didn't have to wait long. I notified the troop that the ambush would be executed shortly. The flares lit up the area, and we blasted away with everything we had, rifle and machinegun fire and the Claymores. We heaved our grenades and then broke contact. Each group made its way to the rally point about one hundred meters away, and we put our backs against a tree, surrounding it in a very tight perimeter. Everyone's eyes were as big as saucers. I listened to hear if we were being chased then called the troop on the radio to tell them our status, that we were OK and at the rally point, and requested pickup at first light, about two hours away.

The troop and Big Al assured me the reaction force would be there, and we verified recognition signals.

The rest of the night passed very slowly. As light returned, we heard the reaction force cranking up. The tracks slowly made their way toward us as we talked them in on the radio. As they approached, we popped a smoke grenade. Big Al identified the color; we linked up and mounted aboard.

The force then proceeded back into the ambush site to assess the damage and check for anything of intelligence value. As we approached we could see the amount of devastation our patrol had caused. Trees and vegetation were shredded, and a red tinge seemed sprayed on the jungle.

We dismounted in the kill zone and conducted a search. There were no bodies to be found but plenty of bloody pieces of flesh. Finally one soldier found something that told us what happened—a boar's foot. We had apparently killed a family of wild pigs!

We suffered unmercifully from the snide remarks of the troop for a while. I like to think those pigs never had a chance, but then, they weren't armed! I still wonder how the pigs knew the song from the *Wizard of Oz*, but I guess being in the middle of the jungle in the dark of night with only a few friendlies around can do funny things to the mind.

Chapter 23

The Hospital

Near the end of my assignment as a platoon leader, shrapnel from an enemy grenade booby trap hanging in a tree wounded me. I had several large pieces of metal in my right thigh that caused moderate bleeding. I wasn't worried so much about the pain as fearful instead that something might have happened to my other equipment in that area. Especially, since I was scheduled to go on R&R to Hawaii and meet Kerry in two weeks, I was very concerned the wound would delay my trip. Luckily, after a quick check, I determined all my essential parts were present and accounted for and ready for duty. Fortunately the squadron had an observation helicopter flying overhead the troop, and the pilot quickly landed to pick me up and take me to the squadron medical aid station.

At the aid station the doctor gave me a quick once-over, stopped the bleeding, then put me on a medevac helicopter to the 3rd Field Hospital in Saigon for surgery to remove the shrapnel. I asked him before I left how serious it was, and would I be transferred out of country. He said I would probably be in the hospital in Saigon for two to three weeks to recover and then be able to return to the unit. I knew the hospital stay would be shorter if there was anything I could do about it.

An old French colonial-era building complex housed the 3rd Field Hospital. The hospital building itself where the patients stayed had open courtyards and a lovely garden surrounded by downtown Saigon. You could hear from the hospital the hustle and bustle of civilian life outside on the streets. I arrived at the hospital's landing pad, examined, and quickly taken into surgery. It must have been a slow day. The doctors used a local anesthetic to cut the shrapnel out of my leg, sew me up and bandage me. Probably the most difficult part of this whole incident was laying waiting for surgery with my pants cut open. As you recall, we didn't wear underwear in the field.

By late in the day I found myself in a ward bed with real sheets and nurses who took good care of me. I had nothing to do but rest up in the hospital. By the afternoon of the second day, I started to walk around, first inside the ward, then around the hospital, and finally the grounds. On one of these journeys of the grounds I observed the activity outside the main gate to the hospital. I had not seen that many people in a long time, and they all seemed to be in a great hurry. The constant noise, the smell of motorbikes, and small cars fighting for the road with bicycles all mixed together. After the normal quiet of the jungle, it appeared frightening to see all this urban commotion.

However, I would soon witness a truly scary event at the hospital.

Every Wednesday night the hospital would show the latest American movies on an outdoor screen in one of its courtyards. Those patients who were ambulatory could go and sit in the courtyard to watch while those who were bedridden were wheeled out on the verandas to catch the movie. A long-time movie buff, I made sure I limped to the courtyard on movie night.

The movie that night, the only one I saw during my stay at the hospital, was *Night of the Living Dead*. In it a group of people hides from bloodthirsty zombies in a farmhouse throughout a long, terrible night. Artillery flares and Spooky gunships (armed C-130 aircraft), firing on the outskirts of Saigon, provided the backdrop for a terrific horror film.

I didn't realize the effect the movie had on me until I got back to my bed. I bent over and looked under the bed to make sure there were no zombies or other ghouls there. I was grateful the light remained on in the ward. I felt like a five-year-old. I was, perhaps, not as frightened as I had ever been in Vietnam, but it was close.

After a little over a week in the hospital, I convinced the medical staff with all my ambling about that I could be released. I had seen the Bob Hope Christmas show on AFVN-TV so Saigon had little else to offer. Besides, I had been writing to my wife for the last week on clean writing paper and mailing the letters in clean envelopes—she might be suspicious that something was amiss. I had not told her I had been wounded, preferring to break it to her directly if and when I went on R&R. I found out later that Kerry's dad had been skeptical about the letters, comparing the ones sent earlier (these were usually smudged in dirt and grime) with these clean ones.

I also wanted to return to my platoon to celebrate Christmas with them before I went on R&R. So I hitched a ride to Blackhorse base camp and flew back to the troop, which had moved in the interim to near the Cambodian border, and arrived there on Christmas Eve.

The platoon had done itself proud preparing for Christmas. The troop had formed a perimeter around a Special Forces camp, and we anticipated a truce on Christmas. Several of the tracks had tinsel, and *Clarence* had a fake Christmas tree. I joined the troops in Christmas carols. At midnight, it seemed every American in Vietnam had saved up green and red star clusters that they fired off into the sky. We had a great Christmas meal on the day itself. I left the next day and headed to Hawaii for R&R.

Chapter 24

Vietnamization

One of the bedrocks of President Nixon's policies for the withdrawal of American troops from Southeast Asia called for "Vietnamization" of the war. Vietnamization meant the turnover of the war effort to the South Vietnamese as quickly as possible. As a consequence, U.S. units could then begin to withdraw. In actual fact, for us it meant very little since we performed the same missions. We now received as replacements soldiers from units being sent home but who still had a lot of time left in country. Coming from one unit to another in a combat zone requires some adjustment, especially if the losing unit had poor discipline.

Despite all the stories you hear about drugs and Vietnam, in the platoon we only had one soldier who failed to understand that his use of drugs put the entire unit in danger. From the time I got to the platoon in mid-June until I was medevaced in mid-December the platoon never left the field except for one short two-day maintenance stand-down at a 1st Infantry Division base camp. While in the field everyone stood guard one two- to three-hour shift every night and watched out for one another all the time. Anyone without all his faculties could leave his buddies in a lurch.

One of these types came to the platoon from a unit going home due to Vietnamization. He had the drawn out look and skinny frame of a drug user and had all types of peace and love slogans drawn on his helmet cover. He wore a beaded necklace to which he attached his dog tags.

Big Al and I would walk our portion of the troop perimeter at night at intermittent intervals. Big Al had a habit of sneaking up on a track from the rear and quietly showing up beside the commander's cupola to see if the person on guard alert or asleep. If they weren't alert, he would cup his left hand under their chin, jerk their head back, and, using the long fingernail he kept on his right thumb, pretend to slit their throat. I have seen more than one new soldier literally soil himself in shock when Big Al used this very effective "waker-upper."

Big Al had performed this maneuver now twice on the new guy and had lost patience with him. He told me he had a solution for the problem and not to worry. I said I'd give him one more chance then recommend military punishment.

The next day the replacement guy's track happened to have maintenance difficulties. Big Al volunteered to stay behind in his track to provide security while the other vehicle's crew worked on repairs. The rest of the platoon moved ahead through the jungle.

While a troop mechanic and most of the crew worked on the "maintenance" problem, Big Al and the new guy went for a walk in the jungle. According to the new soldier later, he must have fallen over several vines and into a tree, because he came back from the walk somewhat the worse for wear. When the two tracks caught back up with the rest of the platoon later, Big Al winked at me. When we had stopped for the day, I found the new guy. He had a black eye and several other obvious bruises. He admitted he had been clumsy and fallen. The platoon had no problems with him again. He also later was awarded a Bronze Start for valor in combat.

Did I mention earlier that Big Al had been the 6th Army boxing champion?

****

The only time I worked with any Vietnamese units during my tour, the troop transported one of their rifle companies on an operation from one town to another. We became essentially bus drivers, and since I spoke no Vietnamese and their company commander spoke no English, if anything had happened to us during the course of the transfer, both units would have been in big trouble. Fortunately, I discovered that their officer spoke French, and with my mélange of French from high school and college we managed to communicate adequately. I still don't think that had a battle broken out, our communication abilities would have worked.

As we travelled about in our area of operations we would see "Ruff-Puffs," the local and regional Vietnamese forces that guarded towns, critical infrastructure, and transportation links. They were not very well equipped and were always looking for hand-outs, but I had to remember that they had been involved in this war for a long time, and they were sitting out at the end of the spear with the expectation of little help. Most were trying to do their best, some undoubtedly were Viet Cong, and I'm sure all were tired since their country had been at war for decades.

Chapter 25

R&R

My bride of barely twelve months met me at Fort DeRussy in Honolulu after a travel story of her own. Kerry had to catch an early morning plane on December 26th but a big snowstorm approached Long Island from the southwest. So Kerry and her family celebrated Christmas Day, and then her father drove her to the airport late that afternoon to ensure she could catch her flight the next morning. He stayed with her that night, then headed home. My father-in-law, Ward Harrigan, is a great guy, even if he is a Navy veteran.

Kerry arrived in Hawaii before me, and settled in the hotel before going to the rendezvous point at Fort DeRussy to meet me. Our plane landed at Hickam Air Force Base, then we took a bus to DeRussy. Still sore from my wounds, especially after riding in the airplane across the Pacific Ocean for hours, I limped off the bus. Kerry bowled me over with a big hug and a wonderful kiss. She had obviously lost weight from worry about me. Then she stood back and looked me up and down and asked about the limp. I told her the long flight had just been difficult.

We went to the hotel and didn't get around to discussing the circumstances of the wounds until other festivities were accomplished for us almost newlyweds. She then noticed the wound scars. Kerry asked about the clean letters and had a thousand other questions. I attempted to answer by simply handing her the Purple Heart medal I had been awarded.

My parents had also come to Hawaii to see their son. Both my mother and Kerry had been extremely worried about me; my dad, who had himself earned a Purple Heart in WWII, had his concerns because they had also received clean letters on Red Cross stationary. We had dinner with them the next day, and I assured them I was in good health, as they could see. We met with them a couple of times the next several days, but they kindly left Kerry and me pretty much alone.

We only had four full days in Hawaii, but we managed to do some touristy things. We rented a small motorcycle to get around, but my shift from combat to the civilian environment caused a problem. Stopping at a light and distracted by all the traffic, I forgot to put my feet down. Kerry quickly hopped off and the bike fell, burning my leg on its muffler.

Kerry and I then had a discussion as to who should drive. I told her I had learned my lesson and persuaded her to get back on. We had no more motorcycle incidents in Hawaii.

The time went very quickly, and we had to say goodbye. Kerry told me she felt better now seeing me in person and knowing I could take care of myself (she has since read some of these stories for the first time, or she might not have been so confident). She said not to worry; she could endure the remaining six months of my tour. My parents also saw me off, and my dad told me to be careful. They took Kerry to the airport later that day for her return to New York. They stayed in Hawaii a few more days on vacation.

Little did my dad or I know the remainder of the tour would prove to be as interesting as the first half.

Chapter 26

The Watch

When I got back from R&R I only had about two weeks with the platoon before moving on to a short stay at squadron as an assistant operations officer. I kept track of U.S. and South Vietnamese unit locations in our area and cleared artillery fire in support of them or okayed harassment and interdiction (H&I) missions. H&I basically meant that, when our artillery felt like shooting out into the boondocks, it could if the area was clear of any friendly units. I would give them a yes or no, and if yes, the artillerymen could go waste some ammunition.

Before leaving the platoon, the troopers got together and gave me a gift Seiko watch from the PX. The gesture touched me. I was truly sad to be leaving them for we had indeed all become brothers. I took some pictures of them, told them I would not forget them, wished them luck, and went off to squadron. The rotation of leadership and the individual troop rotation policy of Vietnam service did not work well. The army has since learned its lesson.

I lasted only two weeks at squadron before becoming the executive officer position of A Troop when that position came open. My responsibility involved running the troop rear, in-processing new troops to the field, and coordinating the daily resupply of parts, ammunition, fuel, food, and water. With the troop clerk, I took care of all the paper work for promotions, awards, and orders for change of station and R&R. I also had to identify bodies coming out of the field, go through their belongings (which were minimal), and write letters of condolence for the troop commander to sign. I visited the wounded if they remained in country and made sure they were ready to return to action. During this time we worked out of the a 1st Cavalry Division (Airmobile) brigade base camp at Quan Loi, eighty miles up the road from Saigon on Route 13.

After I got to A Troop that I found out the gift watch had been purloined, not purchased, from the PX. Nonetheless, it was a fine gift, and I wore it stateside for several years until it broke while I was on a field exercise.

****

The watch incident occurred after an even larger heist. As mentioned earlier, we cavalryman did not envy our infantry brethren's lives very much. The infantry in the 1st Cavalry Division (Airmobile) did, however, have a toy that could make our lives easier.

When we stopped by 1st Cavalry firebases certain of our troopers noticed the infantry had small, all-terrain-type vehicles called 'mules,' a four-wheeled, flatbed transport vehicle about five feet long powered by what was essentially a lawnmower engine. The infantry used the mules at their firebases to transport supplies about or to help off-load helicopters. The troopers wanted one of these handy vehicles.

Our soldiers apparently decided the troop could use a mule for similar purposes and devised a plan to obtain one. During one of our visits to a firebase, the troopers cleaned out the back of an ACAV to make room for a mule. When they had the opportunity, our troopers drove an ACAV over to the mule, dropped the ramp of the ACAV (the entire back end of the vehicle could be lowered) and quickly pushed a mule on board. The perpetrators then closed the ramp, drove off, and the troop left the firebase shortly thereafter.

A day later, as our resupply helicopter came in, the mule suddenly appeared to handle its transport responsibilities. Our troop commander wondered aloud where it had come from and received assurance that it had been "traded" for some enemy weapons we had. That explanation lasted until the radio call from squadron came in telling us to return the mule immediately, that a 1st Cavalry unit was pitching a fit.

The next day we rolled by the firebase and left the pilfered item by the base's front entrance and drove off.

Chapter 27

Cambodia

Three memorable incidents during my tour involved Cambodia. Prior to the May 1970 incursion, Cambodia remained off limits to the American military, at least to regular army units.

The first Cambodian incident took place in late November 1969. The troop was conducted a RIF near the border with Cambodia in an area called the Fishhook. We were told not to get closer than one kilometer from the border and definitely not to cross it. The flat terrain had little topographic features to guide us. The platoon would basically maneuver from savannah-like clearing to clearing, checking out the interspersed jungle patches for signs of enemy activity.

Each platoon had its own zone to reconnoiter and would report back periodically to the troop headquarters. However, knowing your exact location left much to the imagination. We would call in white phosphorous artillery marking rounds that exploded above the ground to orient ourselves. We certainly could have used the inertial guidance device that we had wiped out earlier if we could find any road intersections.

The squadron operations officer in a light observation helicopter flew above the troop's platoons to give us guidance. While he was checking the other platoons we decided to maneuver up a long stretch of open area and come around a jungle patch from the rear. No sooner had we done this and dismounted some soldiers to look at suspicious trails when the helicopter came back and told us to move. We had conducted a mini-invasion (almost a kilometer into Cambodia)!

We remounted and skedaddled back south. We reported our small incursion to squadron, but nothing ever came of it. In the platoon, we liked to think of ourselves as having been in the vanguard of the invasion of Cambodia, only about six months early.

****

The second incident occurred in late March 1970. A Troop had suffered some casualties, including the troop commander, in a fight near Fire Support Base Illingworth, up near the Cambodian border. The troop had volunteered to rescue a trapped infantry company and successfully did so. The troop took shelter at Illingworth the night of the fight, and medevaced its casualties, including the troop commander. The enemy had attacked Illingworth itself a day earlier and it looked in bad shape. I flew out on the resupply bird to take over the troop as the executive officer until squadron replaced me with a captain.

Upon arrival at the fire base, I saw the unit that had been in a tough fight, and a lot of troopers, to include those based out of Illingworth, had "one thousand-yard stares." The troopers were low key but obviously banged up, just like their vehicles. I observed widespread evidence of RPG hits, nicks and dings from incoming weapons fire, and used up weapons. As a side note, A Troop earned the Presidential Unit Citation for the rescue of that infantry company. The award ceremony, however, did not take place until mid-2010.

The troop needed to do a lot of cleaning up and maintenance, but we had little time. The squadron assigned us the mission of pursuing the North Vietnamese soldiers fleeing toward the Cambodian border only a few kilometers away, effective the next morning.

That night resupply took place, and work continued on the vehicles. Early the next morning I walked around with the troop First Sergeant talking about the day's mission and checking out the troop before we departed Illingworth.

I told him I had a weird feeling—that today was the day I was going to die. He listened sympathetically, and then, as any good NCO would, brushed it off as just one of those things. He said he would check on me during the day to see how things were going.

We left Illingworth and departed north, the quickest approach to the Cambodian border and the likely path of retreat for enemy forces. The troop had hardly gone a kilometer into the jungle when a fight started. The retreating enemy left behind a rear guard force to delay our pursuit. The troop deployed, and we used artillery and Cobra gunships to overwhelm the enemy. It wasn't a big fight but did accomplish its mission to delay us. By the time we disengaged and headed north again, the enemy had crossed the border.

During the course of the fight a small piece of shrapnel hit my right hand which flew up and smacked my face. I pulled my hand away from my head, remembering my earlier premonition. I saw it was covered in blood. Maybe my premonition was correct after all—a bad head wound. After a quick moment of panic, however, I realized my hand hurt and not my head, so I carried on with the fight. I must have looked pretty bad, though, because as the action wound down, the First Sergeant came over and looked at me, concerned at the caked blood. When he found out what had happened, he just laughed and told me to "drive on." First Sergeants have a limited supply of sympathy!

****

The last incident involved operations in Cambodia itself after the incursion began. The invasion of Cambodia occurred in May 1970 to destroy enemy supply dumps and root out enemy base camps that were used to support attacks into South Vietnam. Disrupting the enemy in this way would allow President Nixon's Vietnamization program to make progress and permit the gradual withdrawal of American troops from the war.

I would accompany the resupply bird out to the troop's field location every couple of days to coordinate face-to-face with the new commander. The troop commander and I would discuss all sorts of administrative, disciplinary, and supply matters to make sure we were both synchronized.

On this occasion we loaded our internal cargo, to include a replacement trooper and myself, at the troop's rear area. We then flew out to pick up three fuel bladders at a forward location before going on to the troop's field location. The forward pickup point was actually in Cambodia itself.

During this trip, as we picked up the five hundred-gallon fuel bladders, things began to get hairy. The helicopter hovered over the pickup zone to hook onto the three bladders. I could look down a hole in the bottom of the helicopter's fuselage to watch the operation. There appeared to be no problems. I looked toward the front of the aircraft as the pilot applied full power to lift off. Suddenly, the biggest, red, pulsing warning light lit up the cockpit. The synchronization shaft linking the two helicopter rotors had apparently snapped. The two rotors became disconnected from one another and began freewheeling.

The pilot immediately shut down power some fifty feet in the air, and the helicopter dropped like a rock. It bounced on the three fuel bladders, broke its back, fell to the side and split open like a cracked egg. I grabbed the other soldier, and we both dove out of the newly created opening. The two rotors were beating themselves to death, but no fire occurred, either internally or from the fuel bladders. Ironically, twenty-five years later, my daughter married Doug, who became a Chinook pilot.

Later that day I described the incident to Kerry in a letter as "crashing in a helicopter in Cambodia." Since I had less than a month to go on my tour, Kerry waited nervously already. Upon reading my letter, she told her father that I had crashed and captured by the enemy in Cambodia!

Her dad tried to calm her down and read the letter. He finally asked her the pertinent question, "How could he be captured if you have this letter?" Kerry, the junior high science teacher, saw the logic of the situation and reread the letter. She realized that without doubt I would be home in three weeks.

Chapter 28

Fear

As I processed out of the unit's rear detachment, ready to go home, I had the opportunity to consider my tour, and how it had changed me. I had arrived in Vietnam ready to prove myself as a soldier and had done so, despite some very dumb actions on my part. I couldn't wait to get into action, and the first several fire fights proved exciting and confirmed my immortality, even when the dirt from enemy rounds kicked up around me. Gradually, however, I realized that this job could get you killed, especially after I found an enemy bullet lodged in my machinegun's flash suppressor, thankfully caught in mid-flight headed right toward me. Day in and day out we would comb the jungle for the enemy, and over time, the constant nagging fear could grind you down. When would the next track hit a mine, when would we come across an enemy ambush, where would the mortar rounds land, would the night defensive perimeter be attacked? As the time came with fewer and fewer days left in country, those fears rose (giving rise to the question, "How short are you?" followed by the answer, "Why, I'm a two-digit midget" … or … "I could hide behind a dime lying on its side.)"

Really nothing you could do about the fear. Having comrades around in the same situation whom you did not want to let down was the best and perhaps only antidote. You have your duty to do, and your comrades are depending on you. Anything beyond the close horizon of the people on your track or in the platoon I was responsible for wasn't important. As the army puts it and my First Sergeants repeated, when you are afraid you just drive on and rely on your men and your training.

Chapter 29

Stateside

Jet travel has many benefits, the most important being the ability to get somewhere quickly, but there is a downside for soldiers returning from war. It is true for the wars in Iraq and Afghanistan and just as true for Vietnam, the first "quick return" war.

Soldiers returning home from wars in the first half of the 20th Century came back for the most part by sea on troop ships. They then mustered out at stateside camps before returning home, giving them some time to switch to civilian life and decompress. In Vietnam, jet travel allowed you to be in the field one day and literally on America's streets a day or two later. The shock to the soldier's system could be severe, transitioning literally from one world to another in a matter of hours. Couple that transition with the lack of popular support for the war (war protestors spat upon my uniform at the San Francisco International Airport while I waited to fly home) and you found soldiers suffering greatly when they arrived stateside. The army, with these lessons learned, has initiated significant transition programs for soldiers returning from deployments to Iraq and Afghanistan and for their families, but undoubtedly can do more.

Kerry did not have an easy year either. She worried about me in addition to the pressures upon her as a first-year teacher. Often, first-year male teachers, who, despite their lack of education degrees, were teaching to avoid the draft, confronted her. She had sand poured in her gas tank and answered anti-war hang-up phone calls to her home at night. She avoided watching the nightly TV news for fear of what she might see. It did not help Kerry when a West Point classmate's wife would call her and ask, "Have you seen the news?" His tour coincided with mine although we were in different units.

Family support groups did not exist for the families of Vietnam-era soldiers after the first units went over. Vietnam was a one-for-one replacement war, not a unit rotation war. The army has learned great lessons in this area, and it has made a difference in the support structure for families left behind and indeed for the soldiers themselves. Kerry had none of this and, although her family helped a great deal, she had to undergo the stresses with no one nearby in similar circumstances with whom to talk.

One incident in particular scared Kerry and her family nearly to death. A West Point classmate, Dick Scaglione, who had been in our wedding, shipped out to Vietnam about three-quarters of the way through my tour. His family, too, lived on Long Island, and he visited relatives on leave before heading to Travis AFB. He decided to stop in on Kerry and came in uniform.

He parked in front of the house and got out of his car. Kerry spied an army officer from the window and, along with her mother, refused to come to the door when he knocked, afraid that he might be part of a notification team sent to tell her I had died. He stayed at the door and continued to knock, forcing Kerry's mom, Eleanor, to finally answer the door. When Eleanor did and realized who it was, there was momentary relief, followed by concern that he still might be the messenger. Chipper as always, Dick said he stopped to say goodbye before he left and see how Kerry was. Kerry ran to the door, and both she and her mom almost killed him! Then they hugged him and wished him good luck during his own tour.

Chapter 30

Going Home

My tour was up. I had my promotion orders to captain in hand as I said my goodbyes to the troops in the field and at base camp. The new executive officer was in place and briefed. I tried to give Kerry a call from Blackhorse base camp through the MARS (Military Affiliate Radio Station) station. There were obviously no satellite phone or Internet connections. The MARS concept used short-wave radio in Vietnam to tie into a ham radio operator in the states. That operator would then call up the desired party on the phone and link the phone and the radio together. The concept left a lot to be desired with sunspots, dropped calls, and having to say "over," so the person on the other end of the line knew it was her turn to talk. I had little luck getting through to Kerry but at least she got a garbled message I was ready to come home.

Leaving Vietnam produced mixed feelings. I would never forget the comrades, friends, and great soldiers I encountered. My mind had incidents of great intensity seared in it, and the important lessons learned could not be forgotten—they had to be acted upon somehow. I felt a sense of a job left unfinished. I anticipated returning to the Land of the Big PX and the joyous reunion with Kerry. Feeling safe again would be good.

As we boarded the charter jet that would take us to Travis AFB via stops in Japan and Alaska, we found that a CBS television crew would be filming a story on our flight for a news show called *60 Minutes*. The crew would film us as returning veterans just as they had interviewed a planeload of soldiers heading into Vietnam, most for the first time. The interviewer, Mike Wallace, would capture the thoughts of the newbies on the inbound flight to Vietnam and compare them with the veterans on the outbound flight, flights separated by just a couple of hours. The show would air within days of our return stateside after it was edited.

I did not care about the TV show. Glad to be aboard the plane, I just wanted to take off. When the plane left the ground a tremendous roar of relief filled the aircraft, and there was considerable backslapping. I remember distinctly the intense emotions on the plane as that green land faded away under the clouds. I thought the *60 Minutes* crew missed a charged moment when it did not capture the emotion of that take off.

Due to excitement, I did not sleep during most of the flight. I felt cold in both Japan and Alaska during refueling stops, walking around in jungle fatigues. To get some rest, I finally took a sleeping pill for the final leg of the flight into Travis AFB. However, about an hour before arrival stateside, Mike Wallace finally got around to our section of the plane and started his interviews. He had to wake me up to ask his questions.

"So, Lieutenant, what's your first thought coming back the States?"

"Gee, I don't know," I gasped, trying to clear the cobwebs of drug-induced sleep from my brain. "I guess they have to be of my wife … er, good old What's-Her-Name," I sputtered, still trying to wake up. I had forgotten Kerry's name!

Mike asked several other questions that I answered more intelligibly as my mind started to function. Much later, my daughter Megan gave me a DVD of the *60 Minutes* segment for my birthday. As I watched it almost forty years afterwards, all the soldiers appear so young, and they also sound so much alike as Mike interviews them. They not only use the same phraseology, word cadence, and inflection, but the tone of their words indicates great fatigue after a year at war. No matter where we had served in Vietnam or what their combat or non-combat duties had been, the year had obviously taken its toll—we were all just very glad to be going home.

We landed at Travis, processed and made travel arrangements. I got into a Class B khaki uniform. Many of us were bussed off to San Francisco International Airport for flights home. As I mentioned earlier, there was a definite anti-war vibe at the airport towards anyone in uniform. While at the airport, I used the men's room to promote myself to captain.

I went in still wearing first lieutenant rank and traded out my lieutenant's bars for the twin tracks of a captain, very proud of my low-key promotion ceremony in the men's room.

A Marine sergeant had been outside the men's room when I went in and noticed my new rank when I came out a few minutes later. He asked me how I did that. I replied simply that you had to know which stall to use!

****

The transcontinental flight from San Francisco to New York seemed interminable. Kerry picked me up at the airport, and we left for a cabin on eastern Long Island for a couple of days of down time before meeting family. The location was private and quiet, ideal to help me transition from the constant fear of Vietnam in which I had been immersed just a few days earlier. My smart and lovely wife knew the right environment to become reacquainted.

We ultimately stopped on our way to Fort Lewis, Washington, at Kerry's parents and my parents' home in Florida. Kerry's principal had graciously given her early release from her teaching contract to go with me.

My nerves remained on edge, however. A day after arriving in the states we took a walk along a country road when a car drove past. The car backfired not more than twenty meters away. I threw Kerry down as I jumped in a ditch. This reaction did not make her happy, but I'm not sure why—that I emerged from the ditch dirty and soaking wet, or was it my sheepish grin?

****

Before heading to Kerry's home after our stay in the country, I visited Kerry's junior high science classes in uniform. I wanted to thank the children for their support of Kerry and for their efforts sending me care packages. I did not have the heart to tell them that their cookies never, not once, made it to me as anything but crumbs. They really didn't ask me any questions but were glad to see their teacher's husband home. Those children had helped Kerry and therefore me make it through the year. They showered her with going away parties and gifts when she departed the school two weeks early. Their affection and support contrasted completely with the responses a lot of returning soldiers received across the country as they arrived home.

****

Kerry's parents held a welcome home party for me several days later on Long Island to show their pride and to introduce me to all their friends. It coincided with the airing of the *60 Minutes* episode, and they expected to hear what great things I had to say. The Vietnam story appeared on the last segment of the show. The show highlighted several interviews, but no officers were included. We all wondered if I had made the cut when, finally, just before the clock wound down indicating the end of the show, there I was. "I guess it has to be my wife … er, good old What's-Her-Name," then tick … tick … tick, *60 Minutes* ended. Did *60 Minutes* itself have a bias?

Needless to say, I became persona non grata the rest of the party.

Shortly afterwards Kerry and I visited Florida where my parents had retired. As we walked down the road to a nearby beach, a neighbor stopped us. He welcomed me and then asked, "Is this good old What's-Her-Name? I heard about you on TV." I plunged once again into the doghouse.

Finally, after we had reported to our new duty station in Washington State, I received mail from Vietnam from two classmates. They had seen the TV show while waiting at Travis AFB to head to the jungle. They both knew Kerry and one had been in our wedding. They both asked the same question, "How could you?"

****

Now that I had made it stateside, just how could I use the lessons learned in my version of *Hell in the Pacific*?

Part II

The Aftermath

Like many returning Vietnam veterans who opted to stay in the army, I was determined that the lessons I had learned there would be applied to my leadership actions and to pass the knowledge gained onto other soldiers. That resolve directed my efforts with the troops I commanded for the rest of my career whether directly or indirectly.

Chapter 31

Fort Lewis

Kerry and I, after visiting my parents in Florida and assuring them I was in one piece, headed west to our first post-Vietnam assignment at Fort Lewis, Washington. The state-side army was in turmoil, and I was frankly unsure what to expect. The troop withdrawals had started from Vietnam, but the army's focus was rightly still on the war and its requirements.

I arrived at Fort Lewis as a brand-new captain and was immediately assigned command of Charlie Troop, 1st Squadron, 3rd Armored Cavalry Regiment. Charlie Troop was organized exactly like the troop I had just left in Vietnam, so the transition to command was relatively easy. That did not mean, however, command was easy.

I was in charge of over four hundred soldiers, not the usual authorized one hundred and sixty. Many of the soldiers were Vietnam veterans waiting out their final six months or less in the army when they could become civilians again. The rest were new draftees, just out of basic and advanced training, starting their enlistments, and most would go to Vietnam eventually. It was a volatile mix, to say the least.

The veterans weren't about to take anything from anyone and that included the chain of command. Instead of helping new soldiers, many of the vets seemed determined to give them a very hard time.

Thankfully the troop had a seasoned First Sergeant, its top non-commissioned officer. He was a short soldier from Hawaii, known to the troops as Pineapple, but he was a tough cookie. He took me aside on my first day of command.

"Sir," said Pineapple, "I need to tell you a few things, so we can get started out right."

"Go ahead, Top, I'm willing to listen."

"The way I see it, the best bet to keep the troop going is to keep it busy with training and ensure that the old guys pass on lessons learned from Vietnam to the newbies. Use their experience and get them involved—they'll feel more worthwhile and it will help build the unit."

I nodded my head in agreement.

"The troops are going to test you. We need to impose discipline right from the start. As a matter of fact, I want permission to paint two boot prints in front of your desk, exactly one pace, 30 inches, away."

"Hey, wait, Top, what's with the foot prints?"

Pineapple went on. "Sir, there are going to be a lot of Article 15s going on, because the troops will want to know where you stand. I figure painting the boot prints where a troop would stop when called before the commander will give them the idea you're serious about taking command."

"Oh, and one other thing—let's measure the discipline with a little leeway give the good soldiers a break," Pineapple added.

I took his advice to heart, and it was the best thing I ever did at Fort Lewis.

****

The first ninety days in command I administered that same number of Article 15s. The Article 15 is found in the *Uniform Code of Military Justice* and refers to certain limited non-judicial punishments that can be awarded for minor disciplinary offenses by a commanding officer. As a consequence, the boot prints proved invaluable. The troop came to understand that the "old man" (I was twenty-three years old!) was not to be crossed. Pineapple was right, and after a little while the troop settled down. Fortunately, the troop clerk who prepared the Article 15s had a PhD in psychology and was an excellent and speedy typist (remember this was a paper, pre-computer army) and understood what Pineapple and I were trying to accomplish.

At the same time I found rewarding good performance, specifically emphasizing the training of the newbies by the outgoing vets, had great benefits. We regularly granted three-day passes and often there would be sixty or more troops off on a weekend or even during the week.

As regards training, we would go to the field whenever we could because that's where the army operated. Going to the field meant also that you had to prepare to go to the field and recover from going to the field, all of which kept the troops busy and gave time to the non-commissioned officers to teach. Sometimes we would just go to the field for a day, convoying with our vehicles to a distant spot on Fort Lewis, have lunch in the field, conduct some training, then return home.

****

To keep up the troop's enthusiasm for the field, I made a bet with the Bravo Troop commander as to which troop's M114 recon vehicles were best. He and I agreed to have a race between our best M114s on an oval one-mile, cross-country race track to be laid out on one of the Fort Lewis prairies. The race was to take place in two weeks, the length of time our training schedules forecast in the future.

To be frank, the M114 was not the best vehicle the army ever procured. Its lack of reliability was one of the reasons it was never deployed to Vietnam, replaced instead by the more robust M113. It was designed as a lightweight, low-silhouette, reconnaissance vehicle. Though it looked like a sleeker, it was the bane of our existence. It had a solid rubber band track that was always breaking, a gasoline-power Chevrolet 283-hp engine that was too powerful for the vehicle's transmission, and its suspension was suspect. It also mounted a huge 20-mm cannon with more moving parts than you could count!

To participate in the race, we chose the best M114 we had, in reality a choice among real dogs. The troop maintenance section resorted to all kinds of tricks, replacing the track with the newest we could find; tuning up the engine with a high flow-thru air filter, new spark plugs and high capacity carburetor, and a few other tricks. We also took any extra weight from the vehicle (a minimum of gas, one skinny driver, no radios, etc.) We tried out the chosen vehicle on a few stealthy test spins, but still it would not go faster than about thirty-five miles per hour. B Troop was boasting that their track easily topped forty miles an hour.

The day arrived for the big race. We convoyed out as usual to one of the open Fort Lewis prairies and set up the race track with orange cones as the turns. We had our tracks circle the course several times to ensure it was obvious what the course was, then parked all our vehicles motor pool-style near the finish line. It was about ten AM, and the race was to start at high noon.

Since we had time, our M114 and its driver took a couple of spins on the course, and while we were satisfied with his ability to maneuver on the course itself, the damn track still didn't go very fast! We made minor adjustments and continued to wait. By late morning, still no B Troop tracks had arrived. When we questioned the troop commander over the radio, he told us to just hold on, that the troop was on its way. By eleven-thirty, there was still no sign of our competition, and finally just before noon, B Troop called crestfallen and said that it was forfeiting the race.

Disappointed, but also relieved, we had our noon meal in the field on the race course, then departed toward the garrison. We had not gone more than halfway back when we came upon B Troop's race M114 surrounded by its maintenance section. The M114 was actually smoking from its engine compartment, having apparently blown its engine. As C Troop passed on the tank trail, there was much harassment and jeering towards our compatriots in the broken-down M114!

Feeling very good about ourselves, we continued on to the motor pool. Unfortunately, just shy of the gate, our M114 also blew its engine. Hastily, we hooked up tow cables, and masked by a couple of other vehicles, towed it into one of our maintenance bays before any B Troop soldiers could discover what happened.

Charlie Troop rode its success over B Troop for at least a month before word got out what had happened. By then, however, squadron headquarters had banned any M114-racing (or any other vehicle, for that matter), so there was to be no re-match.

****

The troop clerk had a story of his own. As a reward for his hard work fielding all those Article 15s, Pineapple came to me and asked that the clerk be released for sixty days to run for the state senate from Idaho!

It seemed that the troop clerk was a protégé of Frank Church, an Idaho Democrat who served in the U.S. Senate from 1957 to 1981. The clerk was urged by Church to run as a veteran, but the soldier needed more time off than his leave status allowed. Pineapple had done some research along with the clerk and discovered the army had a regulation that allowed sons to return to the farm for seasonal work, i.e., harvesting the crops. It appeared that this provision plus the leave time coming would add up to more than sixty days.

Working with squadron, we received approval of the seasonal work request and sent our boy off to Idaho. He came back a little more than two months later unsuccessful in his election bid but thankful for our effort.

****

My Catholic faith, bolstered by experience in Vietnam, has remained of utmost importance to me throughout my career and in my life. As a consequence and with the opportunities offered in the church as a result of changes brought on by the Second Vatican Council in the mid-1960s, I volunteered to become a lay reader at Mass.

The Fort Lewis Post Chaplain was a Catholic priest and a strict old colonel. He brooked no improprieties at his Masses. Shortly after arriving at Fort Lewis, I was assigned to read at the Main Post chapel, reading from Saint Paul's epistle to the Philippians.

I was a little nervous, for it was to be my first time. Hey, how bad could it be? After all, I had just survived a year in Vietnam. As I strode to the pulpit to read, I nodded at the priest and gave him a hint of a smile. I announced the reading, "A reading from the letter of Saint Paul to the Filipinos."

The priest gasped and stared at me.

Realizing my error, I quickly recovered and announced to the congregation, "I bet you had no idea Saint Paul got that far!" corrected myself, and went on with the reading.

When Mass ended the priest called me over and told me I would not read at the Main Post chapel again. He later relented and even laughed about it, but it was several months before I got back in his good graces and was allowed to read.

Chapter 32

Switzerland

I was in command at Fort Lewis for only 14 months before being reassigned to Fort Knox and attendance at the Armor Officer's Advanced Course, where young captains learned staff functions and how to command. Most of my classmates there had already been in command, and we wondered about the army's timing.

I actually left Fort Lewis early because I was selected as an Olmsted Scholar, based on my academic and army record. The powers-that-be at the Pentagon wanted me to get the Fort Knox course out of the way before heading to my graduate studies in Geneva, Switzerland.

The Olmsted Scholar Program focuses on future leaders in the army. It emphasizes understanding international relations and foreign cultures by having its participants complete two years of study in a liberal arts curriculum in a foreign, non-English-speaking country. As an added benefit, when not attending formal classes, scholars are expected to travel widely.

Once selected, the scholar and spouse, if married, receive extensive foreign language training. Because I had scored well on the army's language test in French (thanks to my classes in high school and at West Point) and because I had actually used my French in Vietnam when working with Vietnamese forces, I was told just to go to the Fort Knox language lab and listen to some tapes to prepare myself for living in Switzerland.

Thankfully, Kerry and I and our new baby, Megan (who was born at Fort Lewis in April 1971 almost exactly nine months after I arrived back from Vietnam), had the opportunity to arrive in Geneva three months prior to start of fall classes at the University of Geneva. This allowed me to take a couple of iterations of "French for Foreigners," presented by the university before starting classes in earnest.

I also enjoyed a couple of other opportunities to practice my language skills during this time. I would walk around Geneva during off-class hours and speak to anyone I could in French. I also bought a Swiss television set and watched the 1972 Olympics whenever I could. The Olympics did amazing things for my multi-sports vocabulary, but soon the real world intruded on these games. The terrorist attack that killed members of the Israeli Olympic Team broadened my international relations vocabulary.

I knew I was ready for fall classes when in September, while walking around Geneva at noon time, I stopped at a newspaper kiosk and engaged the shopkeeper in the news of the day. A stranger tapped me on the shoulder and asked in heavily-accented Alabaman English, "Do you know where the World Council of Churches is?"

"Why, sure," I replied back in English. "Take the Number 3 bus down to its third stop, get off, and climb the hill to the east, and it will be on your right. It's not far away."

"Thank you kindly," replied the American visitor. "You sure do speak English well for a foreigner." He pronounced the word, "furriner."

I went home that night to report the incident to Kerry. She laughed and laughed, but I knew in my heart I was prepared for class.

****

The days in Switzerland went by quickly, and we managed to travel widely—the Olmsted Scholar Program providing wonderful opportunities to encounter different cultures and thinking. Meanwhile, the classes at the University of Geneva were attended by students from all over the world, to include some from behind the then Iron Curtain, and amplified the Olmsted experience.

Since my classmates had eventually found out I was in the army, as we discussed the topics of the day in the school's cafeteria, I would often be accused of being a United States spy. My rejoinder, which seemed to satisfy them, was always, "So who would possibly want to spy on you?"

****

My French was really put to the test late that fall when Kerry, who was already pregnant with our second child when we arrived in Geneva, went into labor. Her OB/GYN doctor spoke English during her appointments, but once the birth process began and Kerry was in the hands of Swiss nurses and mid-wives, all English went out the window. I was pressed into service as a translator and barely got the job done. Happily, our son Colin was born in November 1972 without incident and became known as *"le bebe americain avec un gross tete"* (the American baby with a big head). At almost nine pounds, he was much bigger than the petite Swiss babies.

****

The army was absolutely determined that I should earn my doctorate stateside after finishing up two years in Switzerland, but I was determined to head back to the troops. I argued with the army personnel assignment people that if they left me too long in academia I would forget what it was like to be a soldier. Soldiering was my profession, and it was there I wanted to be. They relented and assigned me to Fort Carson, Colorado.

Chapter 33

Fort Carson

The two years in Switzerland coupled with the time at Forts Lewis and Knox provided me the opportunity to coalesce my thoughts about the lessons learned in Vietnam. The time at Fort Carson provided me with the means to turn these thoughts into action. As I now read General Norman Schwarzkopf's and General Fred Frank's autobiographies, I know the generation of Vietnam officers was doing likewise. At Fort Carson, I served in a tank battalion, for a short while on brigade and division staffs, and finally in the division's 1st Squadron, 10th Cavalry Squadron as its Operations Officer, where I put my ideas into action.

****

The tank battalion gave me lots of opportunity to experiment. After commanding a tank company for a year, I moved to Battalion Operations Officer. The battalion had not done well overall with its tank gunnery program, and I decided to enlist the aid of the Armor School at Fort Knox to make the unit tops in the division.

We conducted eyes tests for all tank crew members. We tested tank commanders, tank gunners and other crew members on hand-eye coordination and the speed with which they identified targets. We arranged other tests through the Armor School that had potential for determining who would be the best tank commander and who the best gunner. We gave them the new Tank Crewman's Skills Test. We looked at all these results, to include a color blindness evaluation, and generated our crew lists. We then, using desk top simulators we borrowed from the Armor School (this was long before the army invested heavily in electronic tank simulators), began to run through hour after hour of dry runs and different scenarios to test various crew pairings. Meanwhile, we had the maintenance folks ensure our tanks and their firing systems were as tight as we could make them. We used loaner boresight devices from Fort Knox to make sure our tank cannons and sighting systems were as close to perfect as possible. We were going the hit the gunnery tables as well-oiled tank crews with the best possible equipment, not show up as individuals for on-the-job training as we had in Vietnam.

We went into the tank cannon firing tables to ensure that all our gunners and tank commanders understood the effects of altitude, ambient temperature, and range on each type of ammunition. We discussed the 'Coreolis effect'—the rotation of the earth under the fired round, tank round propellant temperature, type of ammunition, target speed, wind speed, time of day (was the sun heating the gun tube on one side or the other?), how worn the gun tube was, the effects of firing one type of ammunition after firing another type—called "tube memory," and even the effect of firing the tank from a slant to one side. Our M60 tank gunners and tank commanders became expert in human terms with what would later be handled by a newer tank's fire control computer.

Hence, before going to shoot, for example, a tank commander could tell me that the wind downrange was blowing from left to right at ten miles an hour, so he would have his gunner aim slightly to the left of the center of the target to compensate, all other factors being equal.

With all this technical preparation and personnel management, the live fire training part was actually easy and by the book. The battalion qualified all its crews and was easily tops in the division.

I spent so much time on tank gunnery was it any wonder that nine months after we finished our qualification runs that our third child, Sean, was born. Was it unusual, either, that ultimately he joined the Air Force to fly a tank-killing aircraft, the A-10?

****

A tank battalion relies on its scout platoon to provide it intelligence on enemy movement and to slow down enemy forces to the best of its ability. Because it is such a small unit, it has to rely heavily on its wiles and tricks. Knowing how the enemy used delay tactics and booby traps in Vietnam, we gave the scouts some help. The battalion Chemical, Biological, and Radiological (CBR) NCO showed me how to open up a tear gas grenade and remove the packet of tear gas tablets inside, a packet similar in size and shape to a cylindrical bottle of Alka-Seltzer tablets. This action had to be performed carefully (you had to wear a protective mask, so you didn't get a snoot full of tear gas) but was not dangerous. What it did do, however, is expand your ability to use tear gas against an exercise foe.

Taking the packet apart would yield several tablets of tear gas that one could use in several ways. Simply grind up the tear gas tablets and spread them on a dusty road that the bad guys would use. At the first whiff of tear gas, the unit passing by would have to mask up and report a chemical attack, taking time and focus off its mission. You could tape several tablets to the ignition end of a colored smoke grenade (the tablets were designed to burn anyway). Then, no matter what smoke the enemy unit saw, if it had been caught unawares in the past by tear gas-scented colored smoke, its soldiers would have to put on masks as a precaution, even if nothing was in the smoke. Our scout platoon would often place these make-shift tear gas devices under wooden simulated mines to slow units down. The next time the scouts would just emplace the mines with nothing under them. Finally, tear gas devices hung in trees and pulled out of their hiding places by the antenna of the lead enemy vehicle would cause fits to crews of the trailing vehicles. These techniques were just a variation on a Vietnam theme, only at that time it was used against us. Our scouts could literally hold up an attacking battalion for hours.

****

The divisional cavalry squadron has such a diversity of combat military occupational specialties that makes training its soldiers a challenge. Normally the best live-fire crew training the squadron went through was when its tank crews qualified with the division's tank battalions. While training in this manner was important, I thought it absolutely essential that the various other crews in the squadron also qualify in a similar manner. In their training they should use all the weapons they were expected to employ. They should also be watched as they attempted to qualify by their compatriots in the platoon.

Consequently, based on my experience on brigade and division staff, I was able to convince the folks who ran Fort Carson ranges to turn over two tank ranges in their entirety to the squadron and allow them to be heavily modified to train all the squadron's crews. The crew qualification course tested scout, tank, mortar, infantry, ground surveillance radar, air defense, tank recovery/maintenance, supply truck, aerial rifle, and scout/attack helicopter crews. The crews use their main crew weapon and all the other available weapons on the course as well—machinegun, rifle, pistol, hand grenades, mines, light anti-tank rockets, explosives, etc. I had learned in Vietnam that combat was no time to learn how to use all the combat power the government had given us—do it now in training.

So we set up a variety of targets—tank, personnel, vehicle, and bunker. We also created situations where various members of the crew would react as only they could. For example, as had happened in my platoon in Vietnam, a driver of a track could be called upon to use his pistol to fend off a close-in attack. The drivers loved it as they rolled forward with their vehicles firing their pistols at pop-up targets!

Selected anti-tank missile crews (because of the cost of firing the missile) would fire their missiles at distant targets, then rapidly dismount to fire their rifles at personnel targets, or throw grenades into a nearby bunker. Infantry crews would be given the materials and an hour to prepare and detonate a defensive fougasse device (home-made napalm) or clear a live mine that had been laid by a scout crew on the course prior to them. All the time the crews would be covered by fire from their vehicle's machinegun weapon. Maintenance and combat service support crews would move down the course firing their weapons at targets they could expect to see bypassed by combat elements in front of them.

Mortar crews came under special scrutiny, partially based on my earlier time as a mortar platoon leader and because of the mortar's use in Vietnam. Not only would they use all their personal weapons and the crew machinegun, but they were required while on the course to conduct an indirect fire mission called in by a scout, then conduct a direct lay mission. In a direct lay mission, the mortar crew could actually see the target and by inspection on a map, prepare and fire the mortar rounds on their own and adjust the results onto the target.

To emphasize the air-ground coordination required between the squadron's air cavalry troop and its ground units, pilots became course graders on various tracks. These pilots were not going to mistake a smoking tree trunk for a rocket if I could help it. When it was their turn, flew their aircraft in support of a ground vehicle's attack request. The aerial rifle platoon's infantry squad's would be flown downrange to attack a bunker then be recovered, only to be dropped at the post swimming pool to make a hasty river crossing.

As an important element of the crew qualification course, the squadron used junior enlisted men as monitors at points along the course, for example, the employment of a real Claymore mine. They were all trained on the particular challenge presented. Just as I learned in Vietnam, these junior soldiers were more than capable and lessened the mystery involved in the challenge by their very presence.

Their function was to monitor the crew's preparation and employment of munitions at that point. If they had to step in, these monitors provided peer instruction instead of using a senior NCO or officer. Classes were seldom taught on the range because the crew commanders were expected to have already taught their subordinates the necessary skills to complete the course. As a matter of fact, perhaps the best indicator of the strengths of the course was the individual and small unit attitude toward training. The course was viewed as a challenge, and the variety of situations presented sparked interest in doing the preparatory work. Using live munitions also spurred interest, since the danger factor was always present. Soldiers and their crew commanders were observed researching field manuals and other sources.

The soldiers' enthusiasm for the training showed, and they looked forward to the regular six-month requalification. They practiced their battle drills accordingly and how they would move tactically on targets they knew would be presented to them. They wanted to shine in front of their platoon-mates who watched their progress (and gained intelligence about the course) from the hill behind the range. The top ranked crew in each category was awarded "Top Gun" belt buckles, a source of pride and some preening.

****

Many of the targets used on the crew qualification course range had been erected during my time on division staff in the G-3 Operations section. The division had been offered armored steel aircraft carrier deck plate from the demolition of the jeep carrier *Belleau Wood* at the Philadelphia Naval Shipyard. I jumped at the chance, knowing I would make use of these targets when I went down to the squadron (the G3 was taking over the cavalry squadron, and he wanted me as his Operations Officer)—all we had to do was get it shipped to Fort Carson. The shipyard would cut it up in the sizes we wanted. A train was soon on its way to Fort Carson carrying over six hundred tons of deck plate. Now we had a chance for realistic targets that would show the effects of a round hitting them, not just a hole punched in a wooden target that might or might not be seen through the dust and backblast of cannon fire. Now you could see the bright flash when your round hit steel.

As a matter of fact, as the Squadron Operations Officer, I had the opportunity to fire the first round at one of the steel targets and witness the unmistakable effect of steel-on-steel. Effective training means realistic training. Plus, it's not often you get a chance to shoot at an aircraft carrier with a tank.

****

At the squadron we considered our anti-tank missile training poor. We were equipped with the Tube-Launched, Optically-guided, Wire-controlled (TOW) missile and the army's companion TOW training device, in particular, inadequate. The device consisted of mounting an infrared source centered on a three foot square board on the back of a jeep, sending the jeep to a distant point, then tracking the infrared source as the jeep drove back and forth. The soldier tracking the target was graded on how well he maintained his crosshairs on the target and how much infrared energy he accumulated. There was no firing effect for the launch of the missile or any time of flight calculation for how far away the target was.

The squadron luckily had a tank master gunner assigned to the Operations section. We put our heads together, and we wondered if we couldn't apply some tank gunnery simulation techniques to the TOW training challenge. Eventually, after several Rube Goldberg-like attempts, we developed a TOW simulator system. It consisted of an M-16 rifle mounted onto the TOW launcher tube. The rifle was fitted with an automatic firing device that had been developed with the help of the Electrical Engineering Department at the Air Force Academy (where my next door neighbor was an assistant professor.) The firing device initiated a missile launch pyrotechnic and began a timer to simulate the flight of the missile, at the end of which time the rifle would fire. The target was a scale model tank (also used by tank crews on their own sub-caliber training ranges) on a scaled range. Roughly sixty meters on the range would equal two thousand meters in real distance.

The training sequence went as follows: the TOW gunner would acquire the target and determine if it was in range. He would then fire the TOW (the firing device) while continuing to track the target. The launch signature pyrotechnic would go off signaling the launch of the missile while the soldier continued to track the target. At the correct time, if the soldier was tracking properly, the target tank would be hit by the rifle bullet that had just fired and be knocked out of the way.

In order to better test the feasibility of all this, the master gunner and I would go out into a ditch behind the squadron area (we didn't have time to schedule an entire rifle range for this project), and try out live fire solutions with a borrowed rifle, ammunition, and a TOW launcher. I told the squadron executive officer about this experimentation years after we had both retired from the army, and he almost killed me!

Fort Benning (the Infantry School was the proponent for the TOW trainer) had somehow heard of our work, and the master gunner and I were invited to demonstrate our system there. It worked perfectly, and the school was very interested in adopting it. After all, an M-16 rifle bullet cost only a few pennies compared to launching a real missile. When we got back to Fort Carson after the successful visit to Fort Benning, Hughes Aircraft Corporation (developers of the TOW and its infrared training system) called us and offered the master gunner and me an inordinate amount of money for the idea. "Sorry," we told them, "we've already turned over all the work to the army." Damn!

Ultimately, our training device never caught on since the army, rightly so, was developing electronic simulators that would do a better job than our efforts. If we had not been on the cusp of the electronic age, we would have become famous!

****

While in the squadron, we were on the ground floor in starting up the army's post-Vietnam revival of training on a grand scale, the development of the National Training Center at Fort Irwin, California. The squadron had regularly sent training teams to Fort Irwin to train the California National Guard, so it was somewhat familiar with the post. When the squadron was offered the opportunity to exercise in the desert, we jumped at the chance. We were to be part of a light infantry brigade task force from Fort Ord opposing a mechanized brigade from

Fort Lewis. Fort Irwin at that time held a mystique for most of the army since few of us had ever been there.

****

Three incidents occurred concerning Fort Irwin and remain etched in my mind. In order to ensure the troops were fully prepared and excited about going to the Mohave Desert, we let the word out that this was California after all, and that there were girls behind every tree. As the troops found out, and as we knew, there are few trees at Fort Irwin.

The second incident did involve Hollywood. A television movie production company was at Fort Irwin as the squadron's main body arrived. The company was filming a miniseries called *Ike*, detailing the life of Dwight D. Eisenhower, who commanded American forces during World War II in the European Theater and later became President of the United States. It starred Robert Duvall in the title role and a host of other major league stars.

The producers wanted to use about forty of our soldiers, dressed in period uniforms, as bit players. The movie company erected out in the desert near our assembly area an oasis with a fake pond and plastic palm trees. It was the scene for a picnic with Ike and Kaye Summersby, his driver, played by Lee Remick. Our soldiers, out of camera sight, watched the unfolding of the filming with great interest and ultimately gave the "Hollywood soldiers" a hard time. Once the scene was complete, the movie types carted away the oasis and returned the locale to real desert.

Another Hollywood scene involved the aftermath of the Kasserine Pass, where American troops first encountered the German General Rommel's Afrika Korps. While our soldiers were not used in this scene, we did stumble upon the movie Kasserine Pass battlefield with still smoking tank hulls when the squadron made an early evening move during the field exercise. On one route the squadron drove by a sign that said, "Kasserine Pass, 8 kilometres." Coming across that sign with the burning hulls in the background in our own armored vehicles had an eerie, *Twilight Zone* effect on all.

Finally, since I was the squadron operations officer, I moved all over the battlefield and decided to camouflage my jeep with an M-60 machinegun mount, so my vehicle would look like all our scouts who also drove around in jeeps a la the Rat Patrol.

However, we had a couple of surprises up our sleeves. I had mounted on the jeep's front grill a Claymore mine training aid. The training aid held a flashbulb that, when set off, was supposed to indicate the mine exploding. I also had mounted two smoke grenade launchers from a tank. Since we were often alone, without GPS, and Fort Irwin was so big, there was the chance we could get lost and run into the 'bad guys.' Sure enough, one night while out on a small trail looking for one of the squadron's units, we were halted.

"Who goes there?" came the question, followed by the challenge.

Of course we didn't have the other side's password counter for the challenge and could hear soldiers from the bad guys' roadblock approaching us.

"Put the jeep in reverse, close your eyes, and when I tell you, back up as fast and far as you can," I ordered my driver.

As the 'enemy' neared, I yelled to the driver, "Back up!" then popped the flashbulb and fired the smoke grenades. We rapidly backed up about thirty feet and turned around, never to be seen again.

I will always wonder how the boys from the Ninth Infantry Division reported this incident. I had some of my best times in the army in the 10th Cavalry, and I know the troops enjoyed the training. It confirmed my supposition about army life—you must have the boyish enthusiasm of an eight-year-old if you're going to put up with all the other hardships.

Chapter 34

Fort Leavenworth

Ultimately the army decided to put a stop to my fun and sent me to Fort Leavenworth, fortunately not to the military prison, but for Command and General Staff College (CGSC), to further my military education.

I did what I could to enjoy myself there. The family and I actually arrived early, before the course began, and then we took leave. Since there was no one else in the military housing area at that time, prior to departing we notified the military police to watch after our quarters, one unit in a six-plex. When we returned three weeks later we told the MPs we were back in the house and thank you very much.

The very next night I heard noises downstairs, and suddenly the stairway light went on. I flipped it off and went back into the bedroom to get dressed when I heard footsteps creeping up the staircase. I spun around, crouched in my best Ranger fashion, growled and leapt out into the hallway, as two Military Police (MP), with flashlights extended, rounded the corner. Confronted by this BVD-wearing mad man, they fell back down the stairs to the first landing! Then, composing themselves and drawing their weapons, they switched on the lights again and politely asked me for identification.

"I'm Major Baerman and I'm afraid I don't carry an ID card in my underwear," I replied as calmly as possible.

"Sir," the head MP snickered, "we'll have to take you down to the station."

"Let me get my ID and show it to you, then we can forget about this."

That's what they let me do after a phone call to the station confirming I had earlier indeed notified the MPs my family had returned home.

I'm certain the two MPs laughed through the rest of their patrol about the major in his BVDs and certainly put the incident in their patrol report.

****

That incident was not the last run in I had with the MPs at Leavenworth. All the students were encouraged to participate in intramural athletics between the 16 sections of students at CGSC.

I elected to play soccer, and one afternoon we were playing another team when an Air Force guy tried to kick me in an unmentionable spot. I went down hard but bounced back up and went down the field after him with a full head of steam. I tackled and proceeded to push his face into the mushy playing field. I was pulled off by a couple of teammates and was red-carded by the soccer official. On the sidelines, with my children who had come to see the game all upset, I was questioned by a couple of MPs who, they said, were considering a charge of assault and battery. I argued the 'no harm, no foul' defense (my opponent after all was still in the game and I was not), and it apparently won the day.

****

The MPs at Leavenworth were busy on another occasion. One of my section mates was another Air Force officer who had been a POW in Vietnam and had little love for Jane Fonda and her antics in that war. He apparently had inquired of certain disreputable types in Kansas City, just down the road from Fort Leavenworth, about conducting a hit on Ms. Fonda. The police found out about it and asked the local MPs to question this officer.

The MPs pulled him out of the middle of a class for interrogation. Now this guy had of course been interrogated by some of the best during his prolonged stay in Southeast Asia and was not frightened a bit by our cops. He allowed that he had in fact made low-level inquiries. Our MPs replied that they desired that he cease and desist or things could go badly for him.

He came back to the classroom in good cheer, but we were all over him, asking questions. He told his story, and although a number of us probably would have been willing to support his desires, cooler heads prevailed. The Jane Fonda caper just went away.

****

While at CGSC I was assigned as the sponsor of a Moroccan army major, to help him through the course and help with the translation of certain army terms, since we both spoke French. It was very interesting and doubly educational to see American army doctrine, tactics, and techniques through the eyes of this foreign officer.

One part of the course included an extensive explanation of the Department of Defense supply system, from depot level all the way to the soldier in the field with all the stops in between. The instructor was very good and even passionate in his exposition, affixing magnetic blocks depicting various organizations on a blackboard as supplies made their way to the front. As his class reached a climax, he flipped off the lights and turned on an infrared light source. His magnetic blocks glowed in the dark across the full panoply of the lines of supply. The classroom of officers erupted spontaneously in applause at the effect (or in relief that the class was over.)

My Moroccan friend was perplexed, not only at the complexity and completeness of our supply system but at the reaction of the class. He turned to me and simply said, "Is normal?" Of course, there is nothing normal about the army.

****

The year at CGSC was the 'Year of the Active Defense," an army doctrine designed to counter the Soviet hordes in Europe. We were trying to figure out a way to keep the Soviets from the English Channel since we were so badly outnumbered, and the Reagan defense buildup was still years away. The doctrine was meant to cut the Godless Communists into bite-size pieces while we moved all over the battlefield from one defensive position to another and whittled away at them. It was a very complex and difficult defense to master and would have taken a lot of things going our way to succeed.

In order to help us understand the intricacies of the defense, we would fight battles on terrain models. Rarely would we be successful, so one day, as the commander of that day's battle, I decided to bring out the big guns. My son, Colin, had a toy Godzilla about two feet tall with a spring-loaded fist. A Godzilla of this size definitely dominated this 1:144 scale battlefield. As the Russian tanks and armored personnel carriers poured over the terrain against our defenders, at our final stop line I put Godzilla up on the board and let loose his fist.

He swatted battalions of enemy troops left and right and saved the day. As a matter of fact, if you look in the 1979 copy of the Fort Leavenworth yearbook, you will see Godzilla prominently displayed in all his fury smiting the Commie hordes.

Chapter 35

West Point

I finally arrived to teach history at West Point five years late, thanks to my graduate degree from the University of Geneva. I was unable to delay the inevitable any longer.

I was assigned to the American History Division of the Department of History although my degree was in International Relations. I spent the first summer at West Point becoming acclimatized to the operating procedures in the department and pouring over American history books to get ahead of the cadets.

During my first semester there I found out quickly I didn't have much to worry about. I could call on the assistance of my fellow instructors who were well versed in the nuances of American, especially early American, history. I also found out quickly that my students, freshman cadets called plebes, were interested only in getting the required knowledge in the basic history course poured into their heads and little else.

After about a month or six-weeks into the semester I became a little exasperated with them, so I decided to pull a trick on them. I prepared a special lesson on the Massachusetts colony, specifically on the 'village green' concept by which their towns were organized. I lectured on the layout of the green, the types of stores and houses found there, expounding on the J.C. Penney and Sears stores on the opposite corners, the importance of the telegraph office, and the impact of the bicycle repair shop.

Halfway through my class, I stopped and asked innocently, "Does anything I have said sound peculiar?"

The plebes looked at me in astonishment with wide eyes, "Why, what do you mean?"

"How many of you have read the required reading?"

A majority of them raised their hands. I asked again, "Do you have any questions about what I've said?"

One of the spring butts raised his hand. "I don't understand the point about the bike shop. Can you explain?"

I then proceeded to tell them that in the previous thirty minutes only about the first five minutes had any validity or relationship to the town square. The rest was all made up or yanked from elsewhere on the historical timeline. The cadets looked at me and reacted with surprising anger. They had been fooled and had their valuable time wasted.

I proceeded to tell them that as future leaders and officers in the army, they had an obligation to question things that seemed odd or were just plain wrong. They were expected to think for themselves. Ultimately, we spent the remainder of the class discussing this important leadership value. I then swore them to secrecy about the trick since I had another three other sessions of the same class to teach. To my dismay, all three of those next sessions reacted in exactly the same fashion as the first.

Throughout the rest of the semester I had students questioning what I was saying in class. They kept me on my toes.

I wish the army had our leadership in Vietnam doing the same thing effectively throughout our war years there.

****

I normally taught classes after the noontime meal for cadets. This time period made teaching tough. With the heavy mental and physical load on cadets, some of them succumbed to the arms of Morpheus and, try as they might, would fall asleep. If they did, they were permitted to stand up in class behind their desks until they had recovered. However, there were always a few hard core miscreants. I decided to teach them a lesson.

During my second summer at West Point I volunteered to help at Camp Buckner during cadet field training. In the course of my duties I procured a used smoke grenade and repainted it to resemble a military-issue tear gas grenade. The cadets were familiar with tear gas, having undergone tear gas exposure already during their plebe summer.

I filled the used smoke grenade with sand so that when it was repainted, it both looked and weighed like the real thing. I then placed it on my instructor desk in the classroom and awaited the cadet reaction. When they came in, they immediately recognized it as a live tear gas grenade. Then I told them that if anyone of them fell asleep, the cadet would be required to hold the grenade <u>with the pin pulled</u> until further notice.

Now this situation was perfectly safe (beside the fact that the grenade was a dummy) because if the miscreant kept the spoon of the grenade depressed, the firing mechanism remained cocked, and nothing would happen. If the cadet let go because he or she fell asleep, then it was all over for everyone as the classroom filled with tear gas. Of course, again, there was never any danger of that.

This ploy worked well. The sleepy cadet grew alert, assisted by classmates who didn't want to suffer a tear gas-filled classroom. Some of the cadets eventually started bringing large rubber bands to class, to be used as insurance to wrap around the grenade and hold down the spoon.

My plan worked well until the head of the History Department visited my class one afternoon only to find a cadet standing with the grenade in his hand. After class, when I explained the stunt, he commiserated with my joke and said he appreciated it, but it would be better if I just let the cadets stand as necessary and eliminate the grenade. I explained to all my classes the next day what the grenade really was and why it had to go. The cadets actually seemed a little disappointed because they had had a great time telling fellow students in other classes this particular "war' story.

****

In the middle of my second year at West Point, having recently completed the New York City Marathon and while preparing for another marathon in the spring, I developed insulin-dependent diabetes. I had had a head cold that developed into a chest cold, then dropped lower down. I started to urinate frequently, sometimes barely lasting an hour-long class before rushing out to the bathroom.

I thought I had some sort of urinary tract infection, and after running on a Friday, then weighing myself, and preparing to run on the following Monday, I found I had lost twelve pounds over the weekend! Shocked, I immediately went to the West Point Hospital where the internal medicine doctor tested my blood and told me I had diabetes.

"How can that be?" I asked him. "I don't smoke or drink. I'm in great shape. Here I am preparing for a marathon."

"What does any of that have to do with the fact that your blood sugar is sky high? You have Type I diabetes. Your pancreas is dead," he replied calmly. "Your pancreas was probably killed by a virus. You're just going to have to make some major life-style changes." Later in the 1990s the Veteran's Administration determined that Agent Orange, used in Vietnam to defoliate the jungle, could cause Type II diabetes (the version of the disease whether the pancreas does not produce enough insulin) in exposed veterans. It is still to be determined whether my Type I will fall into the same category.

I was hospitalized, and my blood sugar brought under control. I started taking insulin shots several times a day. Since I was in an academic environment and the doctor did nothing other than note the diabetes in my medical records, I continued on with my assignment. Diabetes, however, was to affect me profoundly through the rest of my career as I tried to keep it under control.

****

The same summer I obtained my dummy grenade, I volunteered for duty with the Recondo Committee, a Ranger-training-lite session at Camp Buckner. In particular, there was a portion of Recondo (a West Point shortening of Reconnaissance-Commando) that took place in the pits, a sawdust-filled arena encircled by sandbags. It was here that the cadets took a short course in hand-to-hand combat, taught by Special Forces soldiers.

Relying on my troop experience and the soldiers I had led in Vietnam, I felt the cadets needed to be pushed hard to be the leaders worthy of the soldiers put in their trust. Therefore, the Special Forces troops and I developed a plan to test the cadets' will.

I addressed the cadet formation as it was about to enter the pits for the first time. "You will learn here more about yourselves today than you could if you climbed the highest Himalayas, spent thousands of dollars, and talked to the greatest of gurus!"

"HOO-AAH!" the cadets yelled back.

"After ten minutes of warm up calisthenics, you will learn the basics of army hand-to-hand and knife fighting. Enter the pits on the double and pair up. NOW!" The cadets rushed the pits and quickly got arranged, facing the center of the arena where a Special Forces instructor on a raised platform began to lead them in exercises. Time passed. Another Special Forces soldier took over and continued the exercises. Minutes passed and yet the exercises continued. Before these exercises began, we made sure the cadets left their watches with their other equipment outside the pits.

Time dragged on until forty-five minutes had passed. Then the instructor on the stand announced, "Now that you're warmed up, we can begin the training!" The cadets let out a collective moan!

The instructor proceeded to teach them a protective stance and, ten minutes later, had them run out of the pits for a five-minute rest period and get a drink from their canteens.

When we had come back in after the rest period, we told them what we had done and why. The lesson learned, we said, was be prepared for anything and be tough enough to outlast adversity. Just as importantly, be good and tough enough for your troops. Hand-to-hand training continued for the rest of the day.

****

It was this same summer I almost resigned from the army. The commander at Camp Buckner had been told by West Point's Commandant, a one-star general, that the general's objective was to have no one that summer quit Camp Buckner and the academy but rather to have fun during summer training. I had always thought training was meant to be tough and, if it was good enough, you had a feeling of accomplishment once it was over. The general had been an Engineer officer most of his career and transferred to Infantry only as a colonel. He apparently had made this move for promotion reasons and had, at least in my estimation, limited time with combat troops, spending most of his time with civil works projects.

During one of our hand-to-hand iterations, a member of the Cadet Counseling Center approached me as I was standing observing the training in the pits. He told me, "Sir, some cadets have come to us complaining how hard the training is in Recondo."

I looked back at the cadet in astonishment, "So what's the problem?"

"Sir," the cadet said innocently, "the Commandant doesn't want to lose any cadets at Camp Buckner."

"And I don't want to lose any soldiers in war!" then I marched off but not before giving the cadet an order to low crawl out of my pits. Down he went and crawled out.

The next day I was called into the Buckner Commander's office. He was a seasoned Infantry full colonel, a veteran of both Korea and Vietnam. "Paul," he said, "I know and agree with what you're trying to do. Can you just tone it down a little?"

"Sir," I replied, "I am prepared to give you my resignation right now if you can tell me I'm wrong." I was worked up about this situation. "If future leaders undergo poor training, the soldiers later under them will undergo even poorer training. Leaders have to be challenged."

"I know, I know," he said. "Just turn the rheostat down a little. I don't want to lose you."

Luckily, we only had two more Recondo cycles to go through before the summer was over, and the cadets returned to the academic year. The Recondo Committee relented a little. Maybe the cadets were a little wiser about what was happening there, but there were no more complaints.

****

I always felt training was the most important thing we do in the army. That philosophy carried over even on my daughter's ninth birthday party. I had set up a picnic in the woods at West Point, complete with cake and drinks and balloons—a normal girl's birthday party.

However, to get to the picnic, I met the birthday party invitees, eight nine-year-old girls, at a parking lot, also in the woods. I paired the girls off, taught them a short map reading class, then gave them maps and four points in the woods to find, with each pair of girls initially heading toward a different point. At the final point, the pair would be directed to the party.

The girls did very well and showed up at the party in a reasonable time with funny stories to tell. Prizes were awarded to the fastest and slowest team, and all got a certificate of completion. My daughter, a West Point graduate herself now, stills tells stories of her ninth birthday party.

Chapter 36

Back to Europe

After the army got its pound of flesh from the Olmsted graduate degree, I left West Point and returned to Europe. The army well on its way to recovery from the throes of Vietnam and, supported by the Reagan build up, was becoming that superb force that demonstrated its prowess in Desert Storm at the beginning of the 1990s.

I was initially assigned as a Brigade Operations Officer in an armored division astride the Fulda Gap. I had been in Germany less than two days and barely met my boss when the alert siren went off at 3AM. The family was asleep in a temporary apartment awaiting our household goods in the building in which we would live for the next three and one-half years. The siren was mounted right above our apartment. When it went off, it shook the entire structure. Never having served in the army in Europe, I staggered out of bed and heard noise in the stairwell. Opening the door, I found my neighbors lugging their alert bags downstairs. I stopped one and asked what I should do, since I had not been issued my field gear yet and had only partially processed into the unit. He said, "None of that matters. When the siren goes off, get going. Report to the Brigade!" I would later learn that the brigade had two hours to 'break the gate,' that is, load up and move out to wartime assembly areas.

Well, this particular alert had an added wrinkle. Once in the assembly area, the brigade commander and brigade staff were supposed to brief the Corps Commander on our war plans at a specific location overlooking Fulda. I had no idea what our war plans were, let alone where exactly Fulda was. The operations staff gave me a quick cram course on our plans because the Brigade Commander, with a twinkle in his eye, had decided against all good judgment in my view, to have me brief the three-star general!

On one of the brigade's battle positions overlooking Fulda and not far from the East German border, we settled in with our easels, map boards, and battle books. I had the opportunity to ask questions and rehearse a couple of times before the sound of helicopters signaled the arrival of the Corps Commander's party. Wearing borrowed field gear and with great trepidation, I muddled my way through the briefing, assisted by the staff and the Brigade commander on particular questions. Luckily it was a nice sunny day and the Corps Commander seemed just pleased to be out of his office in Frankfurt, but I dearly wished I had Godzilla with me! There would be many more opportunities for briefings like this on hilltops in Germany but by then at least I had the knowledge required to give them.

****

I was the Operations Officer and then the Brigade XO for a total of fifteen months, a period that afforded me an invaluable opportunity to learn the army in Germany. It became more obvious to me that the U.S. Army is in fact several different armies, each with its own peculiarities based on location, jargon, local culture, and stresses. One of the reasons the army moves its soldiers around so often is, despite the army's standardization, there is much to be learned and accommodated within each reassignment.

One such lesson learned was Porta-Potty intelligence. The Porta-Potty is of course the mobile crapper. When the army went on field exercises in Germany one of the major logistics feats was proper emplacement of sufficient numbers of Porta-Potties in the right locations to handle the load, so to speak. The Porta-Potties had to follow the flow of the battle.

Consequently, tracking how many Porta-Potties and where they were could give you very good intelligence on the exercise. For instance, a large number of potties concentrated in a small area would indicate an assembly area of a unit. Using a rough ratio of one potty for sixty troops, one could gauge a unit's size. Three potties at an intersection in the German woods meant a company-size unit would eventually show up there. You had better watch out if a bunch of potties showed up on an open flank!

Then there was *brotchen* intelligence. *Brotchen* is the German word for small, hard, delicious bread rolls. Any soldier who has ever been stationed in Germany can tell stories of stopping in his combat vehicle in a German town to go into the local *backerei* (bakery) to get *brotchen* and *butter*. Hence, it was easy to set up roadside stands to sell *brotchen*, stands that were manned by our own U.S. Army and German-speaking scouts in civilian clothes.

Units coming overseas to Germany from stateside on exercise would pull in their vehicles into the stand and ask to buy bread and maybe a *wurst* (a sausage). The stand owner (one of our scouts) would offhandedly ask, in sometimes theatrically German–accented English, "So where in America are you from?"

Since GIs love to talk, the conversation would get started. "I have a cousin near Chicago. How do you like Germany? Where are you going next?" our version of Arnold Schwarzenegger would say. In the course of the sale, it was easy to pick up good intelligence on the unit making the *brotchen* buy with just a few innocuous questions.

****

After my time as a Brigade XO, I was given command of a tank battalion in the same brigade. I wanted to ensure the army knew I was a diabetic, so I went down the autobahn to Frankfurt to the Army Medical Center for a medical review board.

I appeared before a panel of two overweight doctors, army majors of apparent Iranian descent, both of whom were happily puffing away on cigarettes. They invited me to sit down.

"You do know that you can't stay in the army because of your diabetes, don't you?" They had not even attempted to examine me.

"Why is that?" I retorted.

"Because that's army policy."

I looked them straight in the eye. "I tell you what. Let's go out right now and perform the APFT (the Army Physical Fitness Test). If my single score doesn't beat your combined fat-boy scores, I'll give in."

They blustered back and forth. I got up and left, never to see them or their "board" again.

Later that week I wrote my assignment branch chief a letter basically highlighting the incident and received an official letter back wishing me well in my new command.

****

There is a follow up to this story. In my time as a battalion and brigade commander I always had an army medic as my driver. During that time never once did he have to come to my aid, but he employed his skills several times as we came across accidents or incidents requiring medical assistance.

****

In the stateside army you don't get the opportunity to take tanks out on the interstate. In Europe in the 1980s, the autobahn was wide open to us.

After taking command of the battalion, during one alert we added on a tactical movement to a river-crossing site on the Main River near the city of Hanau, not far from our alert assembly area. The battalion scout platoon led us to the site, crossed the river first on their M113 scout tracks (that could float), and secured the far side of the river. The division engineers then put in a floating bridge, and we crossed our tanks. All of this operation was successfully accomplished in a matter of hours. On the way back to the *kaserne* (barracks), we organized in small packets of vehicles and drove on a section of the autobahn.

We had just transitioned from our old M60A3 tanks to the M1, a much speedier piece of equipment. Riding down the road in the right lane at about forty-five miles per hour, we came up on the rear of an old BMW doing about the same speed. As the tank commander up in the tank's turret, I looked over my shoulder and saw that the highway behind me was clear, no German civilian speedster roaring up at one hundred miles per hour. So over the tank's intercom I commanded my driver, "Get in the left lane, and let's go around this guy!"

"Yes, sir!" was his enthusiastic response. I indicated by hand signal (the tank has no turn signals) a left turn and away we went.

"Whoo-eee!" shouted the rest of the crew, the gunner and the loader.

The driver twisted the throttle controls for the powerful turbine engine, and off we flew into the left lane. As we easily passed the BMW, he looked out his driver's window with an incredulous stare—being passed by a tank on the autobahn. Making sure we had plenty of space, we moved back into the right lane. Soon, five other tanks had passed the BMW before we had to exit the autobahn to return to the kaserne. Compared to the same operation we had performed in an M60A3-equipped unit, the M1 took about half the time!

Ultimately we devised a plan to make full use of the tank's power. As part of the brigade's war plan, we had a counterattack mission, one that included a task of crossing the Fulda River with a minimum of engineer support. The scouts could ford the river, but how could we quickly get tanks on the other side to support them?

We reconned the river and found a spot where it narrowed considerably, perhaps only 20 feet wide. If we could build a ramp and get a sufficient run up distance, we could literally jump the river in a tank. The engineer platoon assigned to the battalion built a ramp, and we practiced while we were at one of the army's European training areas. The idea worked perfectly, the M1 leaping some thirty feet, taking off from the ramp at between fifty and sixty miles per hour (we had to remove the engine governor to get up to that speed). The ramp was only good for about four tank leaps before it deteriorated, but that put a tank platoon across the river while the rest of the battalion conducted a more mundane crossing. Of course there were some bruised ribs from hard landings in the jumping crews until we made everyone wear flak jackets to protect themselves.

****

Alerts were always dreaded. You were invariably startled out of a sound sleep, and since they were monthly affairs, the deeper into the month you were, the more likely the alert would occur. Consequently, the more restless your sleep became.

Beside the parade grounds incident, the battalion had three other incidents while breaking the gate. Two involved Volkswagens and contributed to the establishment of the battalion museum.

Our assembly area was not far from the kaserne but getting to it involved a two-lane asphalt road. Tank drivers were given instructions to stay as close to the center of the road as possible to avoid damaging its shoulders. During alerts, with the entire battalion on the move, German civilian drivers were often delayed and attempted dangerous maneuvers.

A yellow VW bug was in a great hurry. Although all our tanks when they moved on German roads had rotating beacons on top of their turrets, the bug's driver came straight toward the lead tank at a high rate of speed. The tank commander directed his driver to slow down and move over but not leave the road. The bug's driver also slowed down but swerved off the shoulder in his haste, then overcorrected and bounced back on the road and into the tank's left track. There are approximately one hundred and sixty track blocks on each tank track, and they each weigh in the vicinity of eighty pounds. The tank itself weighs in the neighborhood of sixty-five tons, so the contest was over before it started.

The tank track grabbed the VW, lifted it up off the ground, and proceeded to chew up the front and right side of the bug. Fortunately for the civilian driver, after being ground up for about 40 feet, the tank track released the car and spit it out onto the shoulder. The female driver was uninjured, her car totaled, and the *Polizei* (German police) cited her for careless driving. About the only recognizable thing we salvaged from the accident was the car's yellow fender.

About two weeks later but on a different, wider stretch of road we had a similar incident with a red VW Passat. This time the German driver continued to speed while approaching a tank convoy and spun out while passing. Again his car was picked up by a tank track, chewed up, and spit out. The involved tank commander never even knew he had been hit by the car and only stopped when the tank to his rear radioed him.

Again, thankfully again no one was injured, but we did obtain a red quarter panel from the Passat. Now the proud owner of pieces of two VWs, I decided to create a battalion museum in the headquarters and began collecting the various artifacts. Individual soldiers were very helpful, donating models of tanks that had been assigned to the battalion and dioramas. Gathered from display cases around the battalion we had WWII German army equipment, historic maps, and battalion trophies and awards. There were even American .50-caliber bullets dug out of the headquarters walls during the fight to capture the kaserne in WWII. We displayed the battalion's route of march across Europe during WWII on a wall mural. There were also more recent acquisitions. Prominent among these latter items were the two yellow and red VW car parts with the admonition to be careful on German roads.

All new soldiers were given a required tour of the battalion museum. Soldiers whose parents were visiting Europe also had the opportunity to visit the museum.

****

A third incident involved an apparently much more skilled driver, this time of a BMW. After the alert ended, the battalion prepared to pull out of its assembly area in the woods. A column of tanks pulled out on to the country road headed home. As each tank entered the road it brought along with it clumps of German mud. Consequently, after six or so tanks had pulled onto the road you had a quarter-mile long stretch of greasy highway. German mud, after centuries of sitting around in well-tended forests, has no equal in its slipperiness.

The tanks all had on their rotating beacons, but the BMW driver was determined to push straight ahead at high speed. No sooner did he pass the lead tank going in the opposite direction than he began to skid on the mud. This driver, however, had his wits about him. First he slid sideways facing the column of tanks, corrected, then slid sideways facing away from the tanks, next backwards down the column, then finally corrected and facing in the original direction of travel, hit dry pavement and, honking his horn, accelerated out of the skid and went on his way.

Those tankers who witnessed this scene were mightily impressed and talked about the incident for months. How this driver could maintain his cool between the edge of the road and a column of 60-ton mudslingers while doing a three hundred and sixty degree skid amazes me to this day.

****

A tank battalion does not have as many different military specialties to train as does a cavalry squadron. Because of the larger number of tankers and the emphasis on tank gunnery, the scouts, mortarmen, and medics often get decreased training emphasis. I was determined not to let them suffer a training shortfall. Consequently the oversight of training for the scouts was specifically given to the Headquarters Company Commander while the mortars became my point of interest, and the medics were trained by the Brigade Surgeon:

- As a highlight of their training, the scouts attended French Commando School and were given other what I like to call 'mind-expanding' missions in the course of their training (see below).
- The mortar platoon was sent off to firing ranges on the average of once a month and often broken down into sub-sections to support two different missions. The platoon was outfitted with special antennas that could be cranked up to increase their radios' range and reliability and also received, as a test unit, the army's first mortar computers to

speed up the unit's responsiveness. The platoon won best mortar platoon in the division, fired seven times their annual allotment of mortar rounds, and over 95 percent of its members earned the coveted Expert Infantryman Badge. When the platoon came back from its final shoot of the year, I had them place brooms in the mount where their machinegun normally would go. I explained to them it was a proud honor, indicating a 'clean sweep' of every task I had set out for them.

Both the mortar and scout platoons completed the Nijmegen one hundred-mile march, and some mortar leaders also went to French Commando School.

- The medics all (one hundred percent) earned the Expert Medical Badge, and many attended both French Commando School as well as marched at Nijmegen.
- All scout, mortar, and medical crews negotiated the same pre-qualification gunnery course (modified according to their weaponry) as the tank crews. The tank recovery crews did the same.

****

Ultimately, however, tank battalions are all about tank gunnery, and we were no different. The tank crew qualification standards in the early 1980s changed significantly and became much more difficult. Consequently, we decided to approach our training a little differently.

Knowledge of the various gunnery scenarios dictated by the new tank gunnery field manual was essential. Hence, we drilled into tank commanders' heads what the scenarios were and how they were to automatically respond.

I would come across a tank commander (TC) and say, "Put on your protective mask, load HEAT!" the same command they would be given on the range (HEAT stood for High Explosive Anti-Tank ammunition). This command meant there would be two armored personnel targets presented. The TC would give me his fire command:

"Gunner!" alerting his crew that a target or targets had appeared.

"HEAT!" instructing the loader to load high explosive, anti-tank ammo in the main gun.

"Two PCs, left PC first!" indicating to the gunner there were two personnel carrier-type targets and which target to fire at first. This command could change depending on which target was closer or presented a greater threat. At this point in the fire command the TC would have control of the main gun and point it in the vicinity of the target he wanted to engage first.

I would reply back to the TC as if I were his loader, "Up!" meaning the main gun had been loaded with HEAT, and the gun safety was off. Now acting as the gunner, I would say, "Identified!" indicating I had acquired the correct target.

The TC would then say, "Fire!" In a real gunnery situation, the gunner would say, "On the way!" then pause a moment to let the crew hang on, and fire the gun. If the first target was destroyed, the TC would engage the second target.

If the TC wasn't quick enough or the fire command was incorrect, down he would drop and give me ten pushups. The rule in the battalion was any tank commander could challenge any other with a scenario, and that meant junior sergeants challenging officers, including the battalion commander. I will admit I both gave out and did a number of pushups.

****

Because there was a lot of stress as tank gunnery qualification neared, I decided that a hand-eye coordination contest was in order. Each tank was issued a green tennis ball with the vehicle bumper number inked on it in magic marker. The contest was meant to keep the crews on their toes. The crew member with the ball could toss it to another crew member who had to catch it on the fly or bounce with his off hand. If the ball dropped, down he went for pushups.

The division commander visited us on the range one evening as twilight turned came across a number of green balls being thrown between tanks as they waited to begin their runs. "What the hell is going on with these tennis balls?" he wondered.

"Sir," I replied, "it's a hand-eye coordination exercise designed to develop the other side of the crewman's brain." After watching us for a while, he probably went away as perplexed as the Corps Commander had with my battle plan explanations my third day in Germany.

****

While we were on the ranges or in the field, the battalion held Family Days. The soldiers' families were bussed out to visit their loved ones in the field, usually a company at a time. Very seldom had they seen their dad or husband doing his job for real. They could watch another unit's gunnery while the soldiers explained what was happening. These days always ended with a picnic in the field, with army rations supplemented by what the families brought. As much time as soldiers spent away from their families, these days proved very popular.

After our field or range time was over, I made sure both single troops and families were given the opportunity to take bus trips to the Armed Forces Recreation Center in Berchtesgarten, Germany. I told the single soldiers that the army had stationed them in Europe and, by God, they were going to make use of that opportunity—no sense wasting a free ticket to Europe then sit around the barracks. Ultimately, almost every soldier and family in the battalion took advantage of these AFRC trips.

****

Although our gunnery training was good, I decided to call in a higher power for an extra edge. Before any tank went down the final qualification course, it was blessed by the battalion's Catholic chaplain. I figured it couldn't hurt, and besides, he prayed for the crew's safety. This same chaplain later was visited by his diocesan bishop in Europe and told that after his tour was up, he had to return as a parish priest to Illinois. The good chaplain was very happy in the battalion and the army and was a great asset. He had in fact on a number of occasions acted as a loader on a tank.

What sealed his fate, however, was his Christmas card later that year back to his bishop. On the front of the card was a picture of an M1 careening toward the camera with the driver devilishly smiling at the photographer. The driver was quite obviously the padre. Topping it off, inside the card was the greeting, "Peace on earth!" Our chaplain returned to Illinois early in the next year.

Whether it was the training, the tennis balls, or the chaplain, the battalion qualified the highest number of tanks in the army in Europe two years in a row.

****

As a battalion commander, I did have my confrontations with brigade and some of the other units on the kaserne. On one particular early alert morning, I had a tank, in its haste to break the gate, tear up a small portion of the kaserne's parade grounds, much to the ire of the Brigade Commander. I apologized, but the battalion was then given the responsibility for the maintenance of the parade grounds.

This responsibility was to last until another unit screwed up, and they weren't about to let that happen. Finally, on the day the Brigade Commander changed command, there was a farewell parade. As my last unit passed in review, I had a soldier marching backwards in the last rank with a bag of seed, sowing it after the unit passed. The new Brigade Commander asked what was going on when I greeted him.

"Sir, this tank battalion doesn't want anything bad to happen to the parade field," I explained. Then I told him how we had gained responsibility for its maintenance. Being a man who could see the humor of the situation and despite being an infantryman, he relieved us of our responsibility and turned it over to the kaserne's infantry battalion. Score one for schutzpah!

****

My son, Colin, however, soon got me in trouble with the new commander. For some reason, the infantry battalion commander decided to populate the old, unused World War II swimming pool in our kaserne with two swans. These swans had clipped wings, so they couldn't fly away; they lived in a little swan enclosure the infantry built. I privately named the swans the first names of the Brigade Commander and his wife since both the swans and the couple seemed quite proper.

My son during this time delivered the European edition of the *Stars and Stripes* throughout the kaserne housing area, to include the Brigade Commander's home up on the hill. One day as he was collecting his monthly charges, he innocently told Mrs. Brigade Commander about the two swans' names, "My dad calls them Wally and Di."

"Very interesting," she replied.

The next day, who was before the Brigade Commander? However, this counseling was not only about the swans, but about the trees the Brigade Commander was having planted around the kaserne by one of my lieutenants, a forestry major in college. I wanted my lieutenant back for gunnery, yet here he was supervising tree planting and maintenance. So I decided to call the project the *Forst* Freeman, after the commander and the German word for forest. Unfortunately, both Colin's incident and the *forst* came together at the same time, and here I was to explain myself. I didn't do a very good job in either case, but I played up the humor and the fact I wanted the lieutenant for training. I did get the lieutenant back, but we also picked up leaf-raking detail, though we did not get the parade ground back.

****

As time neared for my own change of command, a tradition I had started was also going to end. There was a tradition in the tank battalion under the previous commanders that since everyone worked hard during the week, they should party hard on the weekend. This philosophy resulted, sometimes, in an inability by some to perform come Monday mornings. As in any army unit, we had daily physical fitness training, and evidence of readiness or lack thereof was easy to spot. I told the Battalion Sergeant Major he and his NCOs were responsible for getting the week started off correctly and handling any situations that might arise; meanwhile, I would handle the officers on what became quasi-affectionately known as the 'Death Run.'

First thing Monday mornings the officers would report to me in their physical training (PT) clothes. To let them know I was serious about being ready, we would go on some rather rigorous Ranger runs through the woods above the kaserne, to include stops at the obstacle course, sprints, hill runs, chasing after their green tennis balls, etc. Often, in the early days of the Death Run, we would not stop PT until at least a couple of the participants had puked. It became apparent to those who liked to party that there were consequences to their actions. You could do one but not the other, and since Monday mornings were a constant, they quickly had to decide. As a matter of fact, a number of lieutenants reporting in to the battalion told me that they had heard of the unit's PT program while they were in the officer basic course at Fort Knox. Years later I met one of our lieutenants who was now a captain and had commanded a tank company during Desert Storm. He said a Death Run prepared him well for that one hundred-hour fight.

The Death Runs came in a variety of flavors. Near the end of my command, they escalated in terms of scope. Three weeks out from the change of command, we met as usual in front of the battalion headquarters, climbed abroad trucks, and drove out twenty-five kilometers from the kaserne, where we were dropped off. Instructions were given to make our way back to headquarters within four hours without getting caught by the battalion's scouts who were patrolling the roads and pathways in jeeps. In one of the many unusual missions the scouts were given, they could be rewarded with a three-day pass if they captured an officer and returned him to the original truck drop off point.

Two weeks out, again we formed in front of battalion headquarters, then ran down to the parade ground. As we waited, four Blackhawk helicopters swooped in to pick us up and take us fifty kilometers away for a drop off in the German woods. There the instructions said to get back to the kaserne in any way possible using the maps that were handed out, but again, beware of the scouts out to catch the officers. This time the officers were given until early afternoon to complete the return to headquarters. By various means—hitch-hiking, train, etc.—all actually made it, many with real stories to tell!

One week out, that Monday morning was ablaze with rumor as the officers gathered. I had made an arrangement the week before with the Brigade Air Liaison Officer. He called into the battalion duty officer's phone early that morning and indicated that the C-130 aircraft would be landing at the nearby German glider strip as planned. Without further clarification, he then hung up.

Since the officers often gathered around the duty officer's desk before going out for PT, the astonished look on his face made everyone start to ask him questions. When he told them about the phone call, rumors erupted. "The old man is crazy! He's taking us hundreds of kilometers away!"

I arrived shortly afterward, whereupon we completed some warm up exercises. I then announced casually that we were going to run down to the glider strip. Knowing looks flashed across the faces of the assembled officers.

We ran down to the glider strip, across the street from the kaserne. Once there, I put them at ease. I then said that since this was the last Death Run, I had something special for them. You could hear the air being sucked in! There would be no C-130 ride; instead, I awarded each officer a Death Run tab similar to the army's Ranger Tab and told them not to believe in rumors! I told them all to do twenty pushups, then dismissed them back to the kaserne.

Many officers in the battalion wore their unauthorized Death Run tab later that week at the change of command ceremony.

Chapter 37

Hawaii

The family and I were in for a real culture shock with our new orders. I had been scheduled to go in residence to the Army War College in Pennsylvania. At the last moment we were diverted to Pacific Command as an Army War College Fellow. I was assigned as a speech writer for the Commander in Chief, Pacific Command, headquartered out of Camp Smith, Hawaii, in the hills above Pearl Harbor. Talk about a fish out of water—the Pacific, working for an admiral, and living in Navy housing! The entire family arrived in Hawaii in early January in our best LL Bean winter jackets, only to be draped in leis!

****

The assignment turned out to be, however, a terrific educational experience. The downside was the amount of time spent away from home. In the last year of battalion command, I had been away over two hundred days; now, traveling with the admiral, I was gone even more. At least the family had the solace of being in Hawaii, even if it was without Dad.

The admiral's area of responsibility stretched from the east coast of Africa across the Indian and Pacific Oceans to the west coast of the United States. As such, with his busy travel and diplomatic schedule, there were very few countries in the region we did not visit, places American army officers seldom see. The admiral traveled with a small entourage: his executive officer and assistant, a Department of State advisor, two aides, a communications element, a security element, a Navy doctor, a small administrative staff, and me. I spent the majority of my time working on draft speeches. These speeches, that had to be vetted by the State Department, meant a lot of research dealing with the country and/or area in question and how the U.S. national security was affected. The admiral was very effective speaking off the cuff and had a canned speech always ready, so I felt it was a good day if he used a "the" or "but" I had written. If I got an entire phrase in, I was in heaven.

****

On one of our trips to Diego Garcia in the Indian Ocean, I realized how far afield I was. The island of Diego Garcia actually belongs to the British, but we use it as an airfield and as a logistics base to support our efforts in the Middle East. I walked into the Navy's Base Exchange store there in my army Class B uniform and was asked by the store clerk what country's service I was in.

"Why, the U.S. Army, of course," I replied.

"Well, hell, man," exclaimed the civilian, "I've never seen a soldier in here before. Are you lost?"

With stops in Nepal, Bangladesh, Burma (now Myanmar), the Seychelles, the Comoros, Madagascar, Reunion, Mauritius, Brunei, Sri Lanka, Papua New Guinea and most of the islands in the Pacific to include Attu and Kiska in the Aleutians, maybe that civilian was right. Surprisingly, or maybe not given the time frame, I never did get to China, although the trips to Japan, Korea, Malaysia, and Australia made up for it.

****

n one trip we arrived in Manila, the Philippines, shortly after the ouster of President Marcos. The new leadership of the Philippines was anxious to show us what the Marcos family had left behind in its hurry to escape. We toured the Presidential Palace and were taken down into the basement storage area. There we saw row after row of clothes racks, with fashion items and furs, and apparently, hundreds of Mrs. Marcos' brassieres. There were child-size electric Mercedes cars and of course, lots of women's shoes. The tour guide even pointed out the small door that led to a river by which Marcos escaped those who had come to throw them out. I dare say few U.S. Army officers have had the opportunity to tour the Marcos bargain basement.

****

We flew on our excursions in a VC-135, a semi-plush, converted military tanker aircraft with full kitchen, beds, first-class seats, and offices. We flew across the Pacific and Indian Oceans hours and hours at a time. What I, at first, considered luxury soon became a necessity when you considered the admiral's grueling schedule. I was even awarded an air crewman's badge since I spent so much time aboard that airplane.

The admiral's XO was quite a shopper and loved to bring back all sorts of goodies from his trips. The plane luckily had storage space to spare. On a trip to Thailand that the XO did not make, he instructed me to bring back a Spirit House. These houses were made of concrete, intricately decorated, and stood about six feet high on an eighteen-inch square base. The house was meant to provide a home for the spirit that inhabited that particular piece of "Thai land."

I enlisted the aid of the Navy doctor to help me find a spirit house and get it aboard the airplane. We purchased one that was sufficiently gaudy. It came in four pieces, so it could be reassembled like a stack of blocks. I was none too happy indulging the XO's desires and made my feelings known to the doctor. He agreed, but since the XO outranked both of us, what could we do?

When we got back to Camp Smith, we brought the house to the XO's quarters. There he told us to erect it in his yard. I had had enough of his imperious attitude. It was my understanding that a spirit would not live in an incomplete house, so I made sure as the doctor and I were placing the last level on the spirit house to break off one of its roof curlicues. I still don't know if a spirit ever occupied the XO's spirit house.

Chapter 38

Back to Europe Again

Ultimately our time was up in Hawaii after completion of the fellowship, and we headed back to Europe, our familiar stomping grounds. This time, however, it was different kind of assignment. It was to III Corps (Forward), an element of the U.S. Army corps stationed at Fort Hood, Texas but assigned in Europe to the NATO enclave of Armed Forces Central Europe (AFCENT) in Maastricht, The Netherlands. It was the mission of the one hundred or so soldiers in the forward detachment to provide oversight on the equipment, transportation routes, and assembly areas that the corps would use when they deployed to Europe during wartime. In a sense, we were gophers for the corps staff, able to respond quickly when answers were needed to assist in its war planning. Periodically, we would also host elements of the corps staff and its subordinate units when they visited Europe and become tour guides for terrain walks, map exercises, and inspections. At other times we would go back to Fort Hood to participate in exercises there, because we were responsible for and manned the corps' rear area operations center, ready to fight any Soviets who may have penetrated behind our lines.

****

It was a great assignment, especially if you had any appreciation for military history. The corner of the Netherlands where Maastricht was located was within spitting distance of several famous WWII battlefields: the Battle of the Bulge, Hitler's last major offensive; the Hurtgen Forest, a grinding infantry battle in dense woods on the border of Germany; and Operation Market-Garden, the combined airborne/ground assault into Holland to capture crossings over the Rhine.

Maastricht was the first large Dutch city to be liberated by Americans. It was in the Maastricht caves that American soldiers celebrated Christmas in 1944 before heading into the Battle of the Bulge.

****

The forward detachment would often return to Fort Hood for exercises. Since we were a European unit back in the states, we did not have any authorized military transportation. Upon arriving at the Killeen, Texas airport, the local rental car agency gave us a pink Lincoln Continental. We tried to turn it back in for something less ostentatious—there was nothing else available, said the rental agency. We had to get to the exercise.

We quickly named the car the 'pimp-mobile' and went on our way. In the field, needless to say, we couldn't and wouldn't park the car anywhere near our operations center.

The uniform for the exercise called for MOPP-1. MOPP stood for Mission Oriented Protective Posture. It meant wearing an olive drab-colored, charcoal impregnated chemical suit. The suit made the wearer look like a plump ruffian with nothing tucked in, very non-military. As we left the operations center in MOPP after our shift, the fun began. We stumbled about in the dark trying to find the pimp-mobile. My companion fell forward into a barbed wire concertina fence surrounding the ops center. As I attempted to pull him out of the wire entanglement, he ripped his chemical suit in several places on the barbs. The suit issued forth some charcoal powder from its frayed cuts.

The exercise spread across hundreds of miles of Texas and did not actually take place on Fort Hood. We were billeted in a schoolhouse not far away but decided to get some munchies from a local convenience store before turning in. It was after ten at night.

We left our helmets and field gear in the car and went into the 7-11. The lady at the cash register looked at us with fright in her eyes, perhaps because we looked like escapees from the local detention center, especially my fellow with the ripped charcoal suit. We wandered up and down the aisles picking up soda, beef jerky, and chips. Looking over the chip selection, I squeezed a bag of Fritos too hard and it went, "Pop!" with Fritos erupting in a cloud.

The cash register lady yelled, "Take anything you want! Don't shoot me!"

I went to calm her down. "Wait a minute! Don't be alarmed, we're just soldiers."

"Just leave me alone, I don't want no trouble!" she cried.

We slowly backed out of the store, and I threw a ten dollar bill on the floor as we left. We got into our pimp-mobile. I wonder what the Fort Leavenworth MPs would have thought of this incident given my run-ins with the law.

Chapter 39

Northern Europe

Assignment to command an armored brigade in northern Europe was to prove the most difficult time in my career. The assignment after Holland should have been one of the highlights of my career. In one sense of accomplishment it was; in another, it tore me apart. I took command of a forward-stationed armored brigade whose division headquarters was at Fort Hood, Texas in early July. This unit was the only American combat unit in northern Germany. It consisted of two tank battalions, a mechanized infantry battalion, a field artillery battalion, a forward support battalion, a combat engineer company, and a Military Intelligence company, a total of thirty-five hundred soldiers. It was a terrific unit, and I had worked with it often in my job at III Corps (Forward). It was the unit in wartime that assisted in welcoming the rest of the corps when those units deployed to Germany while preparing itself for war.

****

Assignment to northern Germany in the year that the Berlin Wall fell, and Germany began its preparations to reunite, allowed the family and me to travel across the old East-West German border and see what Communism looked like first-hand.

In particular, I wanted to go about sixty kilometers into the former East Germany and look at one of the Soviet kasernes that housed a unit that would have been in the vanguard of an attack against NATO. As we drove further east across the border (just crossing the border was a thrill) the entire family noted how drab the East was—no color, dingy buildings, nothing in the shop windows. Even East Berlin that we had visited years earlier looked good compared to these sights.

We drove into Rostock in our late model Volvo station wagon with U.S. Army Europe license plates. There could be no doubt we were visitors from the West. I had not told Kerry my plans.

I parked the car about one hundred meters from the main gate to the Soviet kaserne and told the family I would be right back. I walked up to the Soviet soldier guarding the gate.

He was from somewhere in eastern Asia, dressed in a huge overcoat with a big Russian fur earflap hat. He was about five and a half feet tall and probably a tank crewman. He probably didn't even speak Russian and certainly not English. I pulled out my army ID card and waved it at him.

"Hey, punk! I'm in the U.S. Army. We would have kicked your ass if you came across the border. I just wanted you to know!"

He looked at me with uncomprehending eyes. I turned and walked off.

Meanwhile, in the car Kerry and the children were having kittens. They were sure they and I were going to be arrested. Visions of a Soviet gulag bounced around in their heads. Nothing further transpired as we turned around and went back across the border. I felt great! It was the highlights in my Cold War experience.

****

It wasn't long after arriving in northern Germany that Saddam Hussein invaded Kuwait, and the army awaited its orders. The first units to deploy were all from the XVIII Airborne Corps stationed at Fort Bragg, North Carolina. The second wave of units ordered in November to deploy came from Europe, to include my brigade. These units would begin arriving in Saudi Arabia starting in January. It was at this time my diabetes raised its ugly head.

Could I deploy to the desert with this disease? The army had little actual experience in the Middle East and I went to my boss and expressed my concerns. As I put it, "I'll die with my boots on," but he was not so sure I should deploy. Kerry was absolutely adamant I would be committing what amounted to suicide. I knew I could fight a war in Europe, but the desert extremes gave me pause. What would happen to me and the unit if I went down?

Kerry and I took some time off and did some real soul-searching and praying. I was insistent I could deploy with some precautions and checked with the local army hospital. The full colonel doctors there were less than enthusiastic and said I would be taking too great a chance with the desert climate. They were uncertain on how to keep my insulin refrigerated and worried about the possibility of losing my insulin in battle or what low blood sugar could do to me. I had to make a decision soon, so if I were replaced, the new commander would have enough time to prepare. Kerry finally confronted me and said the decision wasn't that difficult, it was simple—choose her and the family or the possibility of killing myself, not to mention the effects on the unit.

I made the hardest decision in my career—I decided to hand over command. I wept at that ceremony. There was no change of command parade; I simply handed over the brigade colors in the unit conference room while the brigade continued its deployment preparations. Only Kerry's comfort got me through that day.

I requested that I be allowed to stay at the kaserne to handle the rear detachment responsibilities for all the soldiers' dependents, about four thousand in all. At the least, if I could not directly take care of the soldiers, I could take care of their families. This was granted and all of a sudden, I became the highest-ranking rear detachment commander in Europe, a distinction I little wanted.

****

While the brigade was preparing to deploy, those of us in the rear detachment began our preparations also. I knew one of the most significant things we had to do was counter the rumor mill. We decided the best approach was to overwhelm the families left behind with information and military organization.

Each unit, battalion and company, had its own Family Support Group led by the unit commander's spouse. Those groups had to be kept informed. I tried to encourage any wives from leaving Europe. If they went back stateside while their husbands were deployed they would find little if any military support in their civilian communities and only the local news to rely on. I felt we would be able to help them better with our own resources and up-to-date information in Europe. To those wives who did leave and to the families stateside of soldiers who were deploying, we mailed a newsletter entitled *The Sandblaster* letting them know what was happening at the kaserne and with the deployed unit.

We began a series of classes twice a week in the kaserne's community center about the army: how it fought, how it was supplied, how it communicated, how it handled injured soldiers—from the squad or crew level through brigade. We taught classes on "army-speak" and how the units prepared to go to war. There were classes on what their soldiers needed in the desert and what not to send. Every class ended with a question and answer session that lasted as long as there were questions. These Q&A sessions always started with laying out in the open all the latest rumors, then tackling them one at a time.

The Sandblaster and its staff of two grew substantially as more helpers and writers came forward with suggestions and input. Every other week the group class included a mailing session where volunteers stuffed and mailed out the weekly newsletter. Ultimately, a two-page newsletter grew to a publication of some twelve pages with news reports from the unit, stories about happenings in Germany, poems, pictures, and maps. One of its prominent features was a Dear Abby-like column, called *Ask Desert Debbie*. In it, people would write their letters to Debbie about various concerns, and Debbie would answer. I must confess that I was Debbie and enjoyed the process. I also wrote several letters to myself, asking the kind of questions I wanted or needed to answer!

We also had a radio call-in show on Armed Forces Radio, Northern Germany, doing much the same thing as the classes and Debbie column. Initially, none of these actions received a lot of support, but once the troops were in the desert, we would have hundreds of attendees at the classes, and the mailing list for *The Sandblaster* grew to over four thousand. We needed all the volunteers we could get. We even got the local American high school involved in its production.

****

The Sandblaster was a microcosm of the unit, its families, and the surrounding German community:

- The wife who asked her deployed husband if she would be able "to nurture their children with extra love" and "to take care of her heart, because it went with him."
- Germans who while celebrating one man's birthday surprised an American wife (who had gone to a local *gasthaus* (restaurant) to make arrangements for her Family

Support Group's dinner) by getting up from their seats and saying a prayer for American soldiers in Saudi Arabia.

- Reports back from the desert with cryptic information: "We are not where we were, we are not yet where we are going." In hindsight, the brigade was in the process of making the giant left hook.

- A story about how one of the members of the brigade, a female sergeant, was introduced to a Saudi worker while she was wearing all her combat gear and smoking a cigarette. They shook hands, and the sergeant removed her helmet. The Saudi recoiled in horror, realizing that she was a woman, and then started to lecture her about the evils of smoking. The sergeant calmly retorted, "War is bad, too."

- The local German-American Club members who attended the weekly briefing and distributed bouquets of flowers to the spouses of deployed soldiers.

- The infantry battalion commander who wrote of his soldiers' stamina, character and moral fiber, watching them hand out food, water, and blankets to prisoners of war literally minutes after these same prisoners were active enemy soldiers.

- The humor:
  - Wives wrote that you know you're having a good day when:
    - The commissary has a new shipment of Dove bars
    - Your jeans zip up on the first try, and you're standing up
    - You get a letter from Saudi, and it's less than a month old
  - Wives wrote that you know you're having a bad day when:
    - Your mother-in-law gets mail from Saudi Arabia, and you don't
    - Your husband's buzz haircut looks better than your new permanent
    - Your Dove bars melt on the way home.

- Colored chalk sidewalk art in the military housing area drawn by deployed soldiers' children:

♦   A picture of a baby camel and a dove flying above it
♦   A sign noting "Danger—Minefield Ahead," with a
       pattern of circles drawn across the road followed in
       capital letters by the word, "PEACE!"
•   The Desert Debbie letters asking when is my husband
       coming home.

****

I directly applied one lesson learned from Vietnam to the family support problem. I spent over an hour of every day in the kaserne's commissary. I roamed up and down its aisles talking to the wives there and inviting them to come to the classes and briefings. If they told me they couldn't or wouldn't go, I knew there was a problem and solved it through their Family Support Group. I found just talking to them helped both of us a great deal. I think my interactions in the commissary (after all, everyone had to come there to get food), looking these women in the face, plus word-of-mouth caused the numbers who attended these group sessions to grow greatly. It also helped wives to meet other wives and get things out of their systems. Many of the sessions ended with a group pot luck.

Some of the Q&A sessions could be brutal. There were strong-willed women who had firm convictions about what was going on and held to those convictions despite being confronted with reality. As soon as one rumor was discounted, another succeeded it. I even considered scheduling more than two groups sessions a week. The counter-rumor campaign also included my talks to different Family Support Groups on a daily basis.

****

I remember specifically being called a liar by one wife at the community center and was saved only by a number of wives turning to this woman and shutting her down. On another occasion, the head of a Family Support Group came to me exasperated with the antics of one of her members. She told me that her group had done everything possible to support this spouse, to no avail. She was out of control and causing disturbances throughout unit and the community. I told the Family Support Group head I would handle the problem.

I had painted on the floor before my desk two footprints (sound familiar?). I had the garrison Sergeant Major arrange an appointment between me and the problem woman. The SGM also was to be a witness at this appointment. We choreographed the entire encounter.

The SGM greeted the woman outside my office and told her how to report in a military fashion to me, noting the placement of the footprints. Remember that this woman was the spouse of a soldier and not in the army herself.

She knocked on my office door. In my best command voice I ordered, "Come!"

She entered, stepped on the footprints, and stated her name as the SGM had instructed.

Seated behind my desk, I told her to remain at the position of attention, then proceeded to tell her all the things she had or was doing wrong. I told her we were not having a discussion. I intended to give her an Article 15 (that I was not authorized to do because she was not in the army) and that "I was going to talk, and she was going to listen." I told her that her actions would directly reflect on her husband's career and that I was preparing to ship her involuntarily stateside after I finished the Article 15. I pulled out the *Manual for Courts Martial* and read various parts from it, sounding as official as possible.

Very quickly the tears came, and the SGM handed her a box of tissues while she continued to stand at attention.

Having chewed her up one side, I repeated everything I had said down the other. The woman was literally shaking by this time and never opened her mouth.

Meanwhile the SGM off to her side was doing all he could to keep from smiling.

I ended the dialogue ("I'll talk, and you'll listen") with the admonition that "she was on a very short leash," and if she pushed me at all, "all hell would come down upon her." I then dismissed her, and the SGM led her out of the room.

He also had another part to play as this kabuki dance finished. He told her just how mad I was and that she could be gone, maybe without her children, as soon as tomorrow night. However, if she were to write a letter of apology and ask for forgiveness and volunteer some community service, maybe things could change.

This she did, and we never had a problem from her again.

I wrote her husband and his commander in the desert, and they both thanked me for my actions, illegal though they might have been.

****

As I indicated earlier, sometimes the Q&A sessions were very difficult. Once the war was over, the army announced that units would return from Saudi Arabia and Kuwait on a "first in, first out" basis. This policy meant that the brigade would be one of the later units to return. In preparation for the next weekly briefings, I calculated when the first troops should be arriving back in the kaserne based on the redeployment rate of the XVIII Airborne Corps units.

Sure enough, no sooner had the group session started than the question was posed. I tried to couch my answer with some wiggle room, but the group wanted a date. I finally relented and gave them 9 May and the following days. I finally gained some credence when it turned out the main body of the brigade returned at the end of the first week of May.

There was a wife who had vowed she would not shave her legs until her husband had returned safely from war. Shave them she did, anticipating his arrival, but when the husband arrived home, he found that before he could take his long-awaited shower, he had first to unclog the drain. Even the best of intentions can disrupt homecomings.

****

Taking a break from my duties as rear detachment commander, once the war was over and I knew the troops were coming back, I once again took the family across the border in early spring to see just what had happened to East Germany in the six months since we were last there.

Flowers were growing in the death strip that used to be the border. Roads that were in poor shape before had begun to be patched. Eastern Germans had started to paint their buildings and sweep up like their western compatriots. At a main intersection we had noted during our first trip across, we saw capitalism at work.

A sidewalk café had been set up on one corner with colorful umbrellas, tables and chairs. The chef was making a wonderful goulash soup with fresh brotchen out of an East German Army soup trailer repainted in bright colors of its own. I'm sure the trailer had been stolen, and he was working on his own, but the soup was delicious, the service fine, and it was a beautiful day to be in eastern Germany.

Kerry, however, insisted we not go back and visit our friend in Rostock. It was evident to me from the flowers, the painted buildings, and the soup trailer who had won the Cold War.

****

I met every planeload of soldiers coming back, just as I said goodbye to all who left. With the eleventh and last issue of *The Sandblaster* published, the last family briefing held, and the Family Support Groups disbanded, it was time for my family and me to leave Germany.

Chapter 40

The Last Days in the Army

My last tours of duty in the army were bad fits for me in a number of ways. The Chief of Staff of the Army had visited me in Garlstadt to congratulate me on our rear detachment successes. He also told me that, though Colonels Branch in the army's Military Personnel Center wanted to give me another Brigade-level command in a training unit at Fort Knox, he could not approve that due to my diabetes and non deployability. He explained that it would not be fair to my peers. In essence, he had said I had no chance for promotion—my career was over.

Upon return from Europe I was assigned as Director of Army Command and Control. I was responsible for the software, equipping, and employment of computer-based, automated command systems at the tactical level in the army. While I agreed that the army must go in this direction, I also was convinced, based on what I had seen in similar test equipment used in III Corps exercises, that it was premature to push this equipment to the field. As army historian Brigadier General S.L.A. Marshall had noted in his seminal book, *The Soldier's Load and the Mobility of a Nation*, we, as an army, tended to weigh our soldiers down to their detriment. The computer equipment we had at the time was just too heavy, took too much power, and required too much transportation in the units where it was assigned. We needed to hold off issuing this equipment until it could be downsized. After all, the computer revolution was producing smaller and faster systems in ever decreasing cycles.

I recommended the army wait at least another five years—our software and equipment would be much better then. Unfortunately, my boss did not want to hear this from his Director of Command and Control, and I was invited to find another job. In essence, I was fired, further sealing my fate as posited by the Chief of Staff. I had lasted less than a year in the job.

****

Fortunately for me, one of the people I met in the job was the commanding general at Communications Electronics Command (CECOM), the developers and overseers of the army's computer equipment. Apparently, he and I were not far apart in our assessment of the automated command systems, and he offered me the job of garrison commander at Fort Monmouth, New Jersey, where CECOM was located.

Fate obviously entered in at this point. Kerry's younger sister, Beth, had had a second recurrence of her breast cancer and needed help. She lived near Boston with her husband and two very young children. If we were at Fort Monmouth, we could go to visit her regularly and see our son, Colin, in college in Providence, Rhode Island, as well as our daughter, Megan, finishing up at West Point. After a quick consultation with Kerry, we were on our way to Fort Monmouth.

For family reasons it was a good thing we were there. From a military standpoint, I was an Armor officer on a Signal Corps post. Not only were the military there mostly Signal Corps, but they were in the development and procurement business. Many of them had not been in the real army in quite a while. They worked mostly with civilians and contractors and had their own interpretation of army rules. They were dealing with multi-million dollar contracts (if not more), and some of them could not be bothered by the fact they were expected to be soldiers. Just getting them to take their annual physical training test was a real battle.

****

I knew my time in the army was nearing its end with the hint of scandals surrounding my Commander-in-Chief, President Clinton. These incidents even affected me directly. I had a soldier come before me for military justice for the charge of fraternization, to put it delicately, with a much younger female soldier. In his defense he offered the fact that he had done nothing worse than the President had allegedly done with certain young ladies while governor of Arkansas, facts later confirmed in his second term by the Monica Lewinski scandal. I gave him his due for a novel defense strategy and noted that, while I had no authority over the President, I certainly had and would use my authority over him. I reduced him in grade and fined him, ensuring his career was going nowhere.

That afternoon I made an appointment with the CECOM Commanding General and told him I was putting in my retirement paperwork. After the last couple of years and with the fraternization incident in mind, I said it was best if I retired—the army had stopped being fun.

****

Ultimately, I had what I considered to be the last laugh with the Signal Corps. The army was returning to the states thousands of obsolete tanks. There was an on-going reduction of forces in Europe, an agreement between NATO and the Warsaw Pact countries, a further benefit of the fall of Communism. The army would practically give any municipal authority one of these tanks for a monument on the town square. In fact, many of these tanks were simply pushed off ships on the East Coast to build up reefs.

I arranged for an M60A3 (the type tank I had when I first commanded a tank battalion) to be shipped to Fort Monmouth. I worked with the post engineers to construct a concrete pad near the gate on which to display the tank. Finally the day came when the tank arrived at the nearby civilian rail yard. Unfortunately, no one on post had a tank driver's license but me! Down I went to the rail yard, refamiliarized myself with the tank's driver's compartment and controls, and started it up. Escorted by State and Military Police cars, I drove it on to post and positioned it on the display pad, the only tank within miles.

Of course, I had to give the Signal Corps its due, so the plaque describing the tank also noted it featured radios, computers, and sensors developed by the folks at Fort Monmouth. For me, the main thing was that the tank covered the entrance to the post in an imposing Armor manner.

As I was driving through the post in the tank, I remembered my cadet trip visit to Fort Monmouth when I was a West Point First Classman. The Signal Corps general then commanding Fort Monmouth gave a rousing speech about how "the last person standing and communicating on the battlefield will be the winner!" Impertinent even then, I asked him, "So who will he be communicating with?"

Some things just come full circle.

Epilogue

I've been retired from the army now almost seventeen years, and while working in civilian life, have had the opportunity to reflect on the twenty-six years of service and its acquired knowledge and experience. I've found for civilian life as well as in the army, there are four worthwhile pieces of advice to lead a worthwhile existence.

****

Consider the source. Life is a series of judgment decisions, none more important than those made during crisis, the heat of battle. Part of the decision making process is assessing the validity of the information received and its source. How many times have you received information, only to question the information it contained, who sent the report, on what was it based, how much training and experience did the reporter have, was there any bias? Remember the helicopter pilot that had us check out the smoking rocket when the platoon was on a road security mission?

These sorts of questions evolve into more specific, personal rules of thumb. For me, two examples will suffice. First, in a crisis, never believe the first reports because they're usually wrong. People don't have enough information, don't see the entire picture, or they're just too excited. They want to report something, but not all information is good information. Better to hear them say, "We have a developing situation here," than for them to fill the air with nonsense.

Remember to apply your own experience to what you hear. When I heard someone tell me that their vehicle had broken down but that they'd be back on the road in thirty minutes, I always multiplied this estimate by three and added forty-five minutes. Thus I knew I could expect them, in this case, in two-plus hours. In an office environment, you could use a variant on this theme to set deadlines knowing how your people operate.

By the way, *consider the source* also means listening to your subordinates. Often it is the newer folks who have some of the best ideas, and their input is important to the organization. Hence, a leader/manager ought to be out listening a lot. Walking the perimeter in Vietnam was a great occasion to listen to the troops.

This principle especially applies to one's self. Can those who receive your word trust it completely? What's your track record? Does your word mean something? Once your word is given, do you do everything in your power to ensure the task will be accomplished?

****

Never hire Ms. Buxley as your secretary. Ms. Buxley, General Halftrack's secretary in the comic strip *Beetle Bailey*, may do a good job, but she is a distraction at Camp Swampy. Leaders are expected to be upright and conduct themselves appropriately, focusing on the job. If the leader doesn't do the right thing, how can the organization be expected to do otherwise? When we become leaders, we take on a considerable burden. Our example should mean something, both in our personal and professional lives. Many leaders seem to separate the two when in fact they are inseparable. Focus on your job, and do the right thing. This was stressed at West Point and every moment as an officer. Ultimately the failure of my Commander-in-Chief to do so caused me to retire from the job I loved.

As leaders we are called to a higher standard and should do our best to meet it. The troops in Vietnam wanted their officers to be the best. Leaders should push themselves and those they train accordingly. The Recondo training at Camp Buckner was hard training for motivated and fit cadets. To do otherwise would have been to short change the cadets. Yet there was an effort to approach the training with a lowest common denominator approach. This attempt was simply wrong and could not be allowed. To do otherwise would have corrupted the cadets.

****

Don't pick up anything man-made on the battlefield. There are many ways to look at this principle, but the main one here is the concept of discipline. The army is obviously a dangerous business, but even in the civilian world, when confronted by sights, sounds, and smells of an unknown nature, if you are not trained and disciplined, you can be in trouble quickly. When all hell breaks loose, rely on the standard procedures, drills, and rules to help.

The world can be a nasty and difficult place, and most normal people react to it in dire situations with some degree of shock, even with the best discipline and training. Before, during, and after stressful times, leadership plays an important role. Before the event, leadership preparation is key; during the event, leadership must make the right decisions; after, leaders must make the rounds of their people, look each one of them in the eye, and see how they are doing. He must let them know what has happened from his perspective. He needs to acknowledge that a certain amount of shock is to be expected and prepare his people to continue. An old platoon sergeant taught me long ago that looking into a person's eyes, putting a hand on their shoulder, and getting them to talk is the best medicine.

****

Our reward is not on this earth. My sainted Irish mother would have made this the sole principle. You're put on this earth for some reason, hopefully to make it a better place in the eyes of God. Do this each and every day. I could go on...but that's a topic for another book.

Military Glossary

ACAV – Armored Cavalry Assault Vehicle

AFB – Air Force Base

AFCENT – Armed Forces Central Europe

AFRC – Armed Forces Recreation Center

AFVN – Armed Forces Radio and Television Vietnam

APC – Armored Personnel Carrier

APFT – Army Physical Fitness Test

ARAAV – Armored Reconnaissance Airborne Assault Vehicle

BDA – Bomb Damage Assessment

CBR – Chemical, Biological, and Radiological

CECOM – Communications-Electronics Command

CGSC – Command and General Staff College

CH – Cargo Helicopter

CVC – Combat Vehicle Crewman

FAC – Forward Air Controller

G3 – General Staff Plans and Operations Section

GI – Government Issue

GPS – Global Positioning System

H&I – Harassment & Interdiction

HEAT – High Explosive Anti Tank

ID - Identification

LT - Lieutenant

M1 – Abrams Tank

M113 – Armored Personnel Carrier

M114 – Armored Reconnaissance Vehicle

M16 – 5.56mm caliber Standard Army Rifle

M60 – 7.62mm Standard Army Machinegun

M60A3 – Generation of Army Tanks prior to the Abrams M1

MARS – Military Affiliate Radio System

MASH – Mobile Army Surgical Hospital

MOPP – Mission Oriented Protective Posture

MP – Military Police

NATO – North Atlantic Treaty Organization

NCO – Non-Commissioned Officer

NDP – Night Defensive Position

NVA – North Vietnamese Army

OV-10 – Forward Air Controller Aircraft

POW – Prisoner of War

PT – Physical Training

PX – Post Exchange

R&R – Rest & Relaxation

RIF – Reconnaissance in Force

RPG – Rocket Propelled Grenade

SGM – Sergeant Major

TC – Track Commander/Tank Commander

TOW – Tube-Launched, Optically-Tracked, Wire-Guided

VC – Viet Cong

WWII – World War II

XO – Executive Officer

ISBN 978-0-557-94909-0